MERCER'S
BELLES The Journal of a Reporter

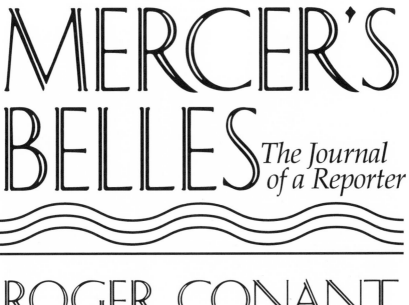

MERCER'S BELLES
The Journal of a Reporter

ROGER CONANT

EDITED BY LENNA A. DEUTSCH
WITH A FOREWORD BY SUSAN ARMITAGE

WSU PRESS

Washington State University Press
Pullman, Washington

Washington State University Press, Pullman, Washington 99164-5910

©1992 by the Board of Regents of Washington State University
All rights reserved
Second printing 1993

Library of Congress Cataloging-in-Publication Data
Conant, Roger, 1833-1915.
　　Mercer's belles : the journal of a reporter / by Roger Conant ;
edited by Lenna A. Deutsch.
　　　　p.　　cm.
　　Originally published: Seattle : University of Washington Press, 1960.
　　Includes bibliographical references and index.
　　ISBN 0-87422-089-0 : $25.00.–ISBN 0-87422-090-4 (pbk.) : $16.95
　　1. Voyages to the Pacific Coast. 2. Conant, Roger, 1833-1915–Journeys–Pacific
Coast (U.S.) 3. Pacific Coast (U.S.)–Description and travel. I. Deutsch, Lenna A.
II. Title. F866.C68 1992
305.42′0972′09034–dc20　　　　　　　　　　　　　　　　　92-20225
　　　　　　　　　　　　　　　　　　　　　　　　　　　　　CIP

To Mrs. Helen Loud Poland

*This edition is dedicated to the memory of
Lenna and Herman Deutsch, equal partners in life.*

FOREWORD TO THE SECOND EDITION

A SA MERCER'S 1866 voyage from New York to San Francisco with a boat-load of young brides for the lonely bachelors of Puget Sound is one of the best-known episodes in Pacific Northwest history. Told and retold, the story has acquired a shiny, polished, well-worn quality. It has even achieved a modern apotheosis: recently, a television series was "loosely"–as they say–based upon it!

The Mercer's "belles" incident remains today, as it was in its own time, a well-known but controversial event. Speculations–some serious, some libelous–swirled around the motives of Asa Mercer himself and those of the women who chose to join his expedition. Like many incidents involving a number of players, it has been difficult to establish the historical truth of Mercer's expedition.

That is why the 1960 publication of Roger Conant's diary, accompanied by Lenna Deutsch's careful research and editing, was so important, and why this re-publication is so welcome. Conant's shipboard diary gave us the fullest account of the members of the Mercer expedition en route to Puget Sound. Lenna Deutsch rounded out the account by asking all the right historical questions and answering as many as she could. Thanks to her, we understand Mercer's motives and the tangle of circumstances that prevented him from carrying through his plan on the grand scale he first envisaged. We glimpse the mixture of attitudes, many of them sarcastic, exaggerated, and downright prurient, that contemporary newspapers exhibited toward Mercer and his "belles." And thanks to Deutsch's diligent sleuthing, we also get the fullest possible account of the history of the expedition's members after they arrived in San Francisco and Seattle.

★ ★ ★

Reviewing the book when it was first published in 1960, the University of Washington's noted western historian, Vernon Carstensen, remarked that this account of the Mercer expedition added to the information already available on "one of the best published incidents in the history of the Pacific Northwest." Yet Carstensen's statement about the event being well understood is true in only one respect—concerning Asa Mercer himself. For something is still missing. Here we have an event organized for women, in which women were the major participants and the focus of attention, yet we lack an extended account of the motives, hopes, and fears of the women themselves.

Why were the women so silent, so (apparently) unable to speak for themselves? To solve the riddle of the women's silence, we can use the tools and insights of women's history, a field that did not even exist when this volume first came out in 1960.

One of the techniques of women's history is to examine the "fit" between notions of appropriate sex-role behavior at a given time and the actual historical circumstances of women's lives. Frequently, there is a gap between the ideal and the reality. One famous 19th century example of this "reality gap" was the social expectation that all "ladies" over the age of 15 would wear tightly-laced corsets, even when engaged in work that made corseting constricting, if not actually injurious to their health. Metaphorically speaking, the Mercer's "belles" were similarly constrained.

The scandal surrounding the Mercer project, and the source of titillation ever since, arose from the belief that the women of the expedition were willing to marry any presentable man who happened to be standing at the end of the gangplank when they disembarked in Seattle. Mercer was always very clear that marriage was the primary motive of the expedition. Struck by the preponderance of bachelors in the Pacific Northwest and the surplus of spinsters in New England, Mercer aimed for the Golden Mean. His approach was practical rather than romantic, and herein lay much of the difficulty.

For the vast majority of American women in the 1860s, marriage was their certain fate, just as it had been for their mothers and grandmothers. In fact, marriage was so overwhelmingly expected that few occupations outside of marriage were considered suitable for women. Teaching had just begun attracting women (at half the salaries paid to men) in the 1840s, and most women teachers were teenaged girls who planned to instruct for only a few years before getting married themselves. The battle to make nursing a respectable female occupation had just been fought in the field hospitals and camps of the Civil War (1861-1865) and the longterm outcome remained uncertain. Clerical work for women became another unintended Civil War outcome, caused by the wartime shortage of male clerks in government offices. But the opportunity to be a "typewriter," as the first operators of the new typing machines were called, still lay in the future. And factory work, in which a number of the Mercer's "belles" had been employed, was much harder and less well paid than in the earlier days when respectable New England farm girls had made the textile mills at Lowell a national model. The other female occupations—domestic service, sewing, laundry work—also paid poorly and lacked any semblance of autonomy or independence. Compared to this limited range of options, most women preferred marriage.[1]

In colonial times, marriage had been a matter of practicality. In the earliest days, parents arranged marriages for their children; but even after that custom ceased, the notion persisted that love occurred *after* marriage, as a result of the companionship and shared work of husband and wife. Common sense dictated that young people avoid obvious marital liabilities in selecting partners—such as the sickly and the improvident—but beyond that there was not much to choose among possible partners. Pickiness or notions of romantic love were not part of the marriage script, although sexual attraction might play a vital role. (In late 18th century New England, historical demographers have discovered, fully a third of all brides were pregnant on their wedding day.) This extremely matter-of-fact view of marriage as an economic and sexual contract that could be made to work with any partner remained the preponderant attitude of poor and rural people throughout much of the 19th century.[2]

The forthright Mercer's "belles" who expected to marry soon after their arrival were examples of this rural mindset. Later in the century the Japanese "picture brides" who came to join their husbands in marriages arranged by their parents in Japan proved equally comfortable with their choices, because they were following established custom.[3]

By 1865, however, newer ideas about romantic love had overtaken traditional American ideas of practicality in marriage. Falling in love, the sentimentalization of sexual attraction, and the expectation of a heightened level of personal intimacy between husband and wife were all aspects of romantic love, which itself derived from a new relationship between the sexes in the growing middle class.[4]

The overlay of romantic love with older notions provoked some amusing confrontations, as the conversation with an Illinois farmer reported by Eliza Farnham in her 1846 travel book, *Life in Prairie Land*, attests:

> ". . .this bride of yours is the one, I suppose, that you thought of all the while you were making your farm and building your cabin?"
>
> "No, I never allowed to get a woman till I found my neighbors went ahead of me with 'em, and then I should a got one right thar, but there wasn't any stout ones in our settlement. . .there was a gal I used to know that was stouter and bigger than this one. I should a got her if I could, but she'd got married and gone off over the *Massissippi* somewhar."
>
> "Did you select this one solely on account of her size?" said I.
>
> "Why, pretty much," he replied; "I reckon women are some like horses and oxen, the biggest can do the most work, and that's what I want one for."
>
> "And is that all?" I asked, more disgusted at every word. "Do you care nothing about a pleasant face to meet you when you go home from the field, or a soft voice to speak kind words when you are sick, or a gentle friend to converse with you in your leisure hours?"
>
> "Why, as to that," he said. "I reckon a woman ain't none the worse for talk because she's stout and able to work. I calculate she'll mind her own business pretty much, and if she does she won't talk a great deal to me; that ain't what I got her for."[5]

As this excerpt shows, the new ideas of romantic love made older notions of marriage seem heartless and crude. And when these notions were voiced by women, they seemed downright scandalous. Thus it could easily happen, as Harriet Stevens found, that a middle class woman in San Francisco could confidently assert that "no respectable woman" could possibly have embarked on Mercer's expedition.

In addition to this class-based conflict of marital expectations, there was yet another gender issue that affected the Mercer women. In an era when women were constantly exhorted to confine their activities to the private and domestic realm of home and family, the newpaper coverage of the Mercer expedition thrust the single women into the public eye. Unwillingly, they became public rather than private women. It is difficult today to imagine how uncomfortable women felt when they ventured into the male-dominated public sphere. For example, when Mrs. J. W. Likens was forced, out of economic necessity, to become a door-to-door book sales-woman in San Francisco's business district in 1871, her self-consciousness was acute:

> Taking...my...order-book in my hand, I started up Montgomery street, call-ing on one and all, up stairs and down, in every room.
>
> Some (men) looked at me curiously, others with pity, and *some few* with contempt, while I endeavored, in my embarrassment, and in an awkward way, to (sell books). They would treat me kindly, and were very polite, with the ex-ception of some few ruffians who seemed to have forgotten "their mother was a woman," and would hurt my feelings.[6]

Aware of the hazards of public argument, most of the women of the Mercer expedition sought refuge in the respectability that encased them as tightly as the corsets they wore. Nothing shows the force of respectabil-ity more clearly than the fact that the only woman Roger Conant writes about freely in his journal is "Pontoon," whom he dismisses as foolish and vulgar. No other women, and especially not the several whom Conant ap-parently pursued with romantic attentions of his own, receive extended treatment in his journal. Evidently, personal commentary was a liberty he did not feel free to take with anyone but the outspoken and improper "Pontoon."

Proper gentlemen did not print words about respectable women. This made the raucous and suggestive newspaper comments about Mercer's "belles" particularly insulting; it was a type of leering male commentary normally meted out by newspapermen only to disreputable women, or to those who stepped out of place. Similar comments greeted pioneering suf-fragist Susan B. Anthony when she undertook a lecture tour in the Pacific Northwest in 1870. Beriah Brown, editor of the Seattle *Territorial Dispatch,* editorialized that "Miss Anthony did not openly advocate free love and disregard of the sanctity of the marriage relation, but she did worse – under the guise of defending women against manifest wrongs, she attempts to instill into their minds an utter disregard for all that is right and conserva-tive in the present order of society." And a former editor of the Olympia *Washington Standard* described suffragists such as Anthony and others of similar beliefs as "a host of old maids and fast women, who to gain notori-ety, accumulate money, or to gratify passions I dare not mention – none but such can believe in women's rights, woman's suffrage, or free love."[7] In the face of these attitudes, no wonder most women remained silent, and how remarkably courageous were the ones, like Oregon's Abigail Scott

Duniway, who did speak out in favor of women's suffrage and other women's issues!

Surprisingly, men seemed to believe that female docility and submissiveness were genuine, rather than the qualities women were forced to assume publicly as badges of respectability. Certainly both Mercer and Conant believed in female docility, until the lively and assertive women of the expedition taught them otherwise. Many of the women of the Mercer expedition were adventurous and independent women; they would not have agreed to come on the voyage otherwise. These qualities were just what was needed – in women as well as men – in the pioneer settlements of Puget Sound. Forced to endure an ordeal by publicity on their journey west, Mercer's "belles" responded with courage, determination, and the silence imposed by the constraints of respectability. But even though they were unable to speak for themselves, thanks to Lenna Deutsch's edition of Roger Conant's diary, we are able to catch glimpses of Mercer's "belles" as they really were, and to understand the reasons for their silence.

SUSAN ARMITAGE

Pullman, Washington
June 1992

Notes

1. Alice Kessler-Harris, *Out to Work: A History of Wage-Earning Women in the United States* (New York: Oxford University Press, 1982), pp. 45-107.
2. John D'Emilio and Estelle B. Freedman, *Intimate Matters: A History of Sexuality in America* (New York: Harper and Row, 1988), pp. 42-44.
3. Sucheng Chan, *Asian Americans: An Interpretive History* (Boston: Atwayne Publishers, 1991), pp. 107-108.
4. D'Emilio and Freedman, *Intimate Matters*, pp. 73-81.
5. Eliza Farnham, *Life in Prairie Land* (New York: Harper and Brothers Publishers, 1846), pp. 37-38.
6. Mrs. J. W. Likens, *Six Years' Experience as a Book Agent in California*, quoted in Ruth Moynihan, Susan Armitage, and Christiane Dichamp, eds., *So Much To Be Done: Women Settlers on the Mining and Ranching Frontier* (Lincoln: University of Nebraska Press, 1990), pp. 39-40.
7. G. Thomas Edwards, *Sowing Good Seeds: The Northwest Suffrage Campaigns of Susan B. Anthony* (Portland: Oregon Historical Society Press, 1990), pp. 101, 107.

FOREWORD TO THE FIRST EDITION

DURING THE spring months of 1954, my wife Lenna and I were doing research in the National Archives in Washington, D.C. As we were explaining to the person in charge of one of the record groups our needs for material on the Pacific Northwest, a very attractive young woman could not help overhearing the conversation. She was Mrs. Edward Poland, of Alexandria, Virginia. While the attendant was getting some records for us, she told us that in her husband's family there was a manuscript of a journal of a young man who had accompanied the second Mercer party on a voyage from New York to the Pacific coast via the Strait of Magellan. The document, she said, was in the possession of her mother-in-law, Mrs. Helen Loud Poland, of Loud Island, Maine, a niece of Roger Conant, the author of this journal. When we mentioned that we planned to work in New England and Canadian depositories, Mrs. Poland suggested that we visit her mother-in-law on Loud Island. This was arranged.

On a beautiful afternoon late in July we visited Mrs. Helen Poland on the island. Because there was no electricity, we could not use our photocopy machine. We therefore suggested that she arrange through her daughter-in-law to have the manuscript microfilmed at the Library of Congress, which would maintain a mastercopy and thereby avert loss of the record if anything should happen to the manuscript. The latter, we suggested, should remain with the family so long as it was a treasured heirloom.

It was obvious that the journal was worthy of publication, so when, after our return to Pullman in the fall of 1954, we were informed that the manuscript had been microfilmed, Lenna suggested that we request the privilege of editing it. Since I could not spare the time from my own research, I suggested that she undertake the assignment. Mrs. Helen Loud Poland generously granted her permission.

After the microfilm copy of the journal had been placed in the Library of Congress, there was some publicity. Mrs. Poland, like the self-possessed woman that she is, "was not at all dazzled by this sudden importance of the Journal." She was concerned only with suitable publication. Her patience in the face of some delays and her faith in our purpose to see that her objective is achieved will ever remain among our most cherished and inspiring experiences. To no one could the book have been more appropriately dedicated.*

HERMAN J. DEUTSCH

Pullman, Washington

---

*The original and a microfilm copy of Roger Conant's journal were made accessible to researchers at the University of Washington Libraries, Seattle, following the original 1960 publication of *Mercer's Belles*.

PREFACE

OCCUPYING an important niche in the history of the Pacific Northwest, the tale of the "Mercer Girls" is real, yet it has been told only partially and with many inaccuracies. Of those best able to record what actually happened – Mr. Mercer and the passengers themselves – only a few of them have left personal reminiscences of the voyage, and these few accounts, regrettably, are fragmentary. It is for this reason that the journal of Roger Conant, "Rod" of the *New York Times,* who accompanied the 1866 Mercer emigration party from New York to Seattle aboard the *Continental* to report it for his paper, is such a significant contribution.

Because initially he had no direct vested interest in the emigration scheme, Conant could witness the day-by-day occurrences with the objectivity of a reporter. He was, however, to remain no mere bystander as he identified himself with the group to such an extent that, at times, he seemed to fancy himself a lord protector of the girls. Understandably, a bachelor in his early thirties was not entirely immune to the many feminine charms that were displayed during the voyage.

Though essentially a narrative of the Mercer expedition, this journal is no less important for its vivid description of a voyage in an early steamship around South America through the Strait of Magellan. Steamers from New York to the West Coast were rare in the sixties when the usual sea route to California was broken by a land trip across the Isthmus of Panama. Conant's account augments those of other contemporary travelers who took the same scenic passage.

Even though the journal is of considerable length, it does not begin to tell a complete story. Naturally Conant was not present at all happenings en route and did not even learn of many events second hand. Moreover, his own personal interests governed the selectivity of his account.

Because of the lack of original source material and because of a ready acceptance of the sometimes uncritical interpretations by nonparticipants, the published accounts of Asa Mercer's expedition are little more precise or complete than those of three quarters of a century ago. There is hardly any evidence that the reports of "Rod" in the *New York Times,* or Conant's similar account of the expedition in *Social Voices,* a church paper in San Francisco, were ever cited by other writers. Certainly there has been no comparison of the two texts. The fact that the authorship of the two versions had not been established might account for this. Since the original manuscript of the journal has come to light, it is now possible to compare all three versions and to relate them to descriptions and interpretations offered by other chroniclers of the expedition.

Complete and adequate studies of the Mercer expedition and of female emigration to the Pacific Northwest remain to be done. The numerous controversies in which Mercer found himself and to which casual reference is sometimes made in the journal will not be resolved until a biography based upon Mercer's personal papers is written.

The original manuscript of Roger Conant's journal is recorded in a paperbound notebook of legal-sized pages, in ink, and in a legible handwriting. Four places on pages 62, 65, 131, and 132 were covered over with later entries pasted in, and the original entries could not be read.

A few idiosyncrasies in Conant's writing should be noted. When referring to himself, he uses the plural pronouns such as "we" and "us." He consistently misplaces the apostrophes in contractions, as in "had'nt." These have been corrected. It is difficult to distinguish capitals from small letters, and the small a's, o's, and u's look much alike. Throughout the early pages of the manuscript, Conant uses the term "virgin" when he is referring to the unattached ladies, distinguishing between them with the adjectives "younger" and "elder." In the *Times* version and that in *Social Voices,* he resorted to the more prim "maidens" and "ladies" for the term "virgin."

Where Conant's misspelling of words seems mere carelessness in writing, these have been corrected, but words that he consistently misspells or in which a misspelling is obvious have been left as he wrote them. Quotation marks have been added in many places, since Conant is inconsistent in his use of them. All in all, the journal is well written and is comparatively free of errors in grammar or inelegancies in style. I have supplied chapter divisions and headings.

This book would not have been possible without the generous cooperation of Mrs. Edward Poland and Mrs. Helen Loud Poland, and it is a matter of deep regret to us that Mrs. Edward Poland did not live to see the published journal.

There are many others to whom I am indebted. Particularly to the directors and staff of the various libraries and depositories visited do I wish to extend my thanks for friendly and efficient assistance. Among these are the state libraries of Washington, Idaho, Oregon, and California; the library and archives of the province of British Columbia; the libraries at Washington State University, the University of Washington, and the University of California; The Bancroft Library at Berkeley, California; and the Widener Library at Harvard University. I also appreciate the assistance of the Seattle Historical Society, the Seattle Public Library, New York Public Library, the Santa Cruz, California Public Library, and the state historical societies of Washington, Oregon, and Idaho.

To those friends who read the rough draft, to others who from time to time suggested valuable leads, to those who responded promptly to letters of inquiry, and to the many people who sustained me with their interest and good wishes, I am especially appreciative.

To my son-in-law Bruce C. Harding, who took time from his professional work to search in distant depositories, I extend special thanks.

The person who has been of the greatest aid to me in the preparation of this manuscript has been my husband Herman. When work was going along smoothly, he let me proceed alone and at my own pace, but whenever I felt lost or my natural abilities seemed less than adequate, he was always ready to drop his own work to give me the needed encouragement, to think of an apt word or phrase, or even to point out to me the direction in which I should be going. It speaks well of his patience that his help was always thoughtful and kindly. I appreciate this more than I can say.

To all who have granted permission to use quotations from manuscripts or published works, or to reproduce photographs, I am deeply grateful. These include: The Marine Historical Society, Bancroft Library, Seattle Historical Society, University of Washington Library, Washington State Historical Society, *Pacific Northwest Quarterly, Oregon Historical Quarterly,* the Daughters of the American Revolution, Mr. D. C. Pearson, Mr. Vernon Carstensen, and the Metropolitan Press, Portland, Oregon.

LENNA A. DEUTSCH

Pullman, Washington

CONTENTS

MERCER'S BELLES

The Journal of a Reporter

INTRODUCTION

The Emigration

M ERCER ON US!" This headline in the *Alta California* on April 20, 1866, heralded the eagerly awaited arrival at San Francisco of the S.S. *Continental* and with it, "Mercer's Belles."[1] San Franciscans always seemed to enjoy the unusual as well as the commonplace, the bohemian along with the fashionable;[2] it was not strange that the citizens of this cosmopolitan city evinced much interest in the female emigration scheme of Asa Shinn Mercer.

On April 24, when the ship was anchored to a buoy off Folsom Street,[3] the passengers received a rousing welcome from the swarms of people, trying in vain from wharves and small boats to get on board[4] for a glimpse of the "Genus Crinoline."[5] The curious had to await the morrow when the ladies finally were permitted to go ashore. As the women proceeded along the street to their hotels, the Fremont House and the International,[6] they were highly incensed when they saw displayed in the shop windows some cartoons poking fun at them. Conant later commented:

> The ladies have not formed a very exalted opinion of the San Francisco artists, and they think they might have employed their time to a much better purpose than drawing caricatures of them. As soon as we heard the story, we started down Montgomery street to see these remarkable drawings, and found in one of the windows two large pictures — one representing the "Continental" coming up the bay, completely surrounded by boats filled with men, their arms extended towards the ladies on board the steamer, who in return, were waving their handkerchiefs to the men in the boats. The other represented a man running

at the top of his speed, with a large party of the "Continental" ladies at his heels. A note of explanation at the bottom stated that the ladies were searching for a man, and having caught sight of one, were vieing with each other to see who could secure him first. We told them they must expect (coming in the manner they did) such slurs from artists who had nothing better to do.[7]

But more perplexing to the ladies were the comments to the effect that they were looked upon, at least by some citizens, as women of questionable repute.[8]

This female emigration project, as envisioned by the young bachelor of Washington Territory, was genuine and was conceived with high hopes and purposes.[9] During the decade of the 1860's, there was little visible increase in the population of the territory,[10] made up largely of lonely bachelors of all ages. The few women in residence were, for the most part, married. Even young girls of thirteen and fourteen were betrothed, some to men old enough to be their fathers.[11] Loneliness was merely one of the factors contributing to the desire for more women in the territory. The Donation Land Act, providing grants of 640 acres of land to a man and wife, prompted many a young man's thoughts to turn eastward in search of a suitable companion to share life's pleasures and vicissitudes in this beautiful and bountiful Puget Sound country "where men are wondrous cheap and women are so dear."[12] Those who had someone in mind and possessed the means went east to claim their brides, but there were only a few who could afford the expensive round trip or who could take time enough from their pursuits to make the journey.[13] Some of the men took Indian women as mates, either by marriage, or under a semimorganatic arrangement, and Mr. Mercer viewed this as detrimental to the moral tone of the community.[14]

Because the Civil War had cut down many young men, there were reportedly, in the New England states alone, some thirty thousand unattached women, many of them unemployed because the mills had closed, or widows and orphans without any means of livelihood.[15] The surplus of women in the East was coupled with a scarcity in the West. As president of the infant Territorial University at Seattle,[16] young Mercer was keenly aware of the great need for teachers and wives.[17] Thus he was prompted to attempt remedying the situation on both Atlantic and Pacific coasts by a plan of female emigration. There were grave objections to the whole idea, but the novelty of it seemed to have disarmed many who otherwise might have been critical.

In 1864, acting as an unofficial emigrant agent, he had gone east and persuaded eleven young women (mostly from Lowell, Massachusetts) to accompany him to Puget Sound where they became teachers in the territory's schools or married.[18] Encouraged by the success of his first effort, he thereupon conceived of female emigration on a grandiose scale. This time he planned to return with hundreds of women who initially might find employment as school teachers, seamstresses, housemaids, and the like, but who eventually would marry and rule over territorial households.[19]

Accordingly, he wrote to Governor Gibbs, of Oregon, seeking cooperation and financial aid and inquiring if that state could use some of these women as teachers.[20] On March 1, 1865, shortly before he departed for the East, Mercer entered into a contract with a number of young men of the Seattle area in which it was agreed that he would bring a suitable wife of good moral character and reputation for each man paying him the sum of three hundred dollars, which would defray the passage of said ladies from the East and also compensate him for his trouble. Mercer, likewise, carried east with him other money entrusted to his care by friends and relatives, but for purposes other than the promotion of emigration.[21]

Prior to leaving Seattle, Mercer had discussed his idea with the territorial governor, William Pickering, and with some fellow members of the legislature. He solicited their aid and received encouragement and at least some moral support. Later, in December of 1865, the governor received a dispatch from Mercer from New York which asked for the loan of three thousand dollars. As the governor had no private funds at his disposal, he at once approached the legislature, then in session, for an appropriation. The proposition was favored, but the public treasury was empty and public credit fully 50 per cent below par. The vote was eight for and eighteen against.[22] Though Mercer failed in the effort for official territorial aid, there must have been individual promises of money. This is attested by ". . .we hear it stated that the Governor is about to enforce the collection of certain subscriptions so liberally made by certain members of the last legislature to aid the Mercer scheme. The list will be given to an attorney for collection."[23] It appears these collections were not too successful.

Conant revealed Mercer as a man of many facets, some praiseworthy, some not. Others close to Mercer, in fact Mercer himself, suggested plausible interpretations. Harriet Stevens, one of the girls, said,

> I now believe that only the most conscientious determination not to awaken hopes that would not be realized has led Mr. Mercer to give the impressions of Seattle far below the truth. There is much more of comfort and refinement than I expected. But the one thing above all others with which I am satisfied is the complete justification of Mr. Mercer's expedition which I find in the

facts stated publicly by Rev. Mr. Bagley. It is unfortunate that times have changed since the beginning of the enterprise but surely that is no fault of Mr. Mercer's.[24]

Mercer, when asked many years later to tell something of the venture, replied in part:

> I was at sea without a compass. Drowning men catch at straws. I was the asphyxiated individual and caught at the extended straw. Mr. Holladay had two good lawyers pitted against an inexperienced youth, over anxious and ready to be sacrificed. . . . Later—too late—I saw where the "little joker" came in.[25]

The judgment of C. B. Bagley (son of the Reverend Daniel Bagley) seems to have been objective but understanding. He cites a telegram sent by Mercer from San Francisco to the Rev. Bagley which read, "Will you and Horton authorize Phillips to sign indemnifying bond with me for two thousand dollars?" Bagley continues,

> The guaranty asked for in the telegram appearing above was not sent, but instead a dispatch was sent to Mr. Mercer authorizing him to use funds that had been entrusted to his care by Mr. Bagley for another purpose. This did not afford the anticipated relief, for those funds had been used by Mr. Mercer months before. Right there was the secret of Mr. Mercer's failure at that time and at other times in his life. He was ever prone to take whatever he urgently hoped for as certain of accomplishment. When he had been promised the ship he took all else for granted. Large sums of money had been put into his hand by relatives and friends for certain purposes. All these he diverted to the immigration scheme, and the failure of the enterprise made it impossible for him to pay back these monies. . .That he used these monies for his personal benefit no one claimed, but the fact that their monies had gone toward the accomplishment of the immigration scheme did not reconcile to their losses those who felt they had been robbed by Mercer.
>
> In all the earlier stages of his great work he had not been actuated by mercenary motives. He believed that his mission was one of immense benefit to the territory and of great good to those whom he might induce to come out here. His every action, his whole attitude toward those who had entrusted themselves to his guidance and care was that of a chivalrous, pure-minded American gentleman.
>
> The years that have elapsed since then have verified and justified his predictions as to the far reaching and beneficial effects that were to result to the immigrants themselves and to the new land of their adoption. They have proved a blessing to every community from the Cowlitz northward to the boundary line. In public and at the fireside their teachings and their example have conserved the well-being of the people of which they and their children have formed an integral part.[26]

One of the most extensive personal accounts left by Asa Mercer was an interview that appeared in the *San Francisco Examiner.* It was definitely reminiscent in character and was prepared over a quarter of a century after the event took place.[27]

When it became known that Mercer had gone east again to recruit female immigrants for Washington Territory, the newspapers in the Northwest and elsewhere eagerly featured the story. Charles Prosch, editor of the *Puget Sound Herald*, may have had the explanation for such a response when, a few years later, he recalled that news with human interest appeal had been so scarce that even a neighbor's new picket fence made good copy.[28] The tenor of comments reflected the editors' varied enthusiasms or, perhaps more precisely, what the editors thought would strike the fancy of their subscribers. Headlines were particularly colorful, such as "The Anxious and Aimless" and "Hegira of Spinsters." By the more fanciful, the girls were dubbed "Petticoat Brigade," "Wives for the Wifeless," "Cargo of Heifers," or "Sewing Machines." The disdainful referred to them as "Mercer's Victims," "Consignment of Emigrants," "Cargo of Females," or merely "Female Emigrants." One editor called the project a "Mercer-nary Adventure."[29] The "soles" of the population would be looked after by a dozen shoemakers, wrote an editor with a practical turn of mind,[30] and Mercer, himself, was called the "Moses of this 'Exodus of Women' to Washington Territory" by *Harper's Weekly*,[31] and "Humbug Mercer" by the San Francisco *Morning Call*.[32]

The Mercer female emigration from its inception had been a study in contrasts. The whole idea was treated sympathetically on the one hand, with disdain on the other; people had faith in it or were openly cynical; editors treated the news as fact or embroidered the rumor; the humor was kindly, sympathetic, sometimes malicious, and on occasion very cruel, but most of it was just good-natured raillery.

The *New York Times* reflected a sympathetic understanding of Mercer's aims and purposes as is evident in this paragraph:

> But whoever they are, and whencesoever they come, it is certain that those gentle pioneers go out to the West with a high sense of purpose to which they are devoted, and with hopes educated and purified by the adversities attendant upon the efforts of women at self-help in the East.[33]

Some Massachusetts newspapers were not so kind to Mercer. The *Springfield Republican* was quoted: ". . .and it may well be doubted whether any girl who goes to seek a husband is worthy to be a decent man's wife, or is ever likely to be."[34] This may have prompted the *Times* to reveal that

> The local newspapers of Massachusetts did not favor him [Mercer]; and some of the people thought him a curious individual with a curious scheme; they accused him of seeking to carry off girls for the benefit of miserable old bachelors; and they threw their influence against him and all that he did. These persons ridiculed the women who were willing to go to Washington Territory. . . .[35]

Confirmation of this came later when a Boston weekly, the *Commonwealth*, after the expedition was completed, chided some of the other papers of its neighborhood in this vein:

> Some of the carping journals in these parts that so unjustly assailed Mr. Mercer's Washington Territory emigration scheme, find themselves suffused with mortification at finding that Mr. Mercer acted in a most honorable and generous manner towards every individual who engaged to be of his party.[36]

The *Commonwealth*, from the outset, expressed faith in the project and urged young people to join.[37] It even promised not over a three month's wait until all girls would have the best of husbands.[38] Governor Andrew, Edward Everett Hale, and Rufus Leighton endorsed the scheme, and Hale, who had sponsored a girl already in the West, said she earned thirty dollars a month in gold.[39]

Reporting a lecture in the city of San Francisco, the *Alta California* said, "Miss Anna Dickinson, the pythoness in petticoats...took occasion to pitch somewhat savagely into the affair which she regarded very much in the light of humbug." She wondered, if the women were going west to teach, as Governor Andrew of Massachusetts had indicated, whom would they teach? "How your Washington bachelors can be fathers is a subject rather for a hearty guffaw than for any serious debate."[40]

Though many editors reported the affair as straight news, others indulged in fanciful musings. The editor of the *Walla Walla Statesman* particularly was profuse in his biting ridicule. One example:

> ...it will not be long before the bevy of Massachusetts damsels, armed with green reticules, blank marriage certificates and photographs of Ben Butler to hang on the andirons to keep their babies out of the fire, will be going aboard a vessel and bounding over the watery reflections in search of a market for their kisses. We envy Dr. Mercer. See him standing on the poop-deck, bathing in a sea of loveliness as the invisible hand of sea-sickness leads the *retch*-ed beauties below and him to reflection ....Relics of maidenhood, farewell; may you find the market stiff, and happy hours where the sun goes down.[41]

When he ran out of ideas of his own, the Walla Walla editor quoted from papers published elsewhere. From the *LaCrosse Democrat*, for example, he excerpted,

> The surplus sweetness of Massachusetts spinsterhood is soon to be wasted on the desert air of W.T. for the relief of territorial bachelors who now darn their buckskin breeches and d− −n their hours of solitude....Dr. Mercer...has arrived in Boston and perfected arrangements to return at once with a cargo of Bay State Virgins, in black stockings, candlewick garters, shirt waists, spit curls, green specs, false teeth, and a thirst for chewing gum.[42]

The fertile imagination of the editor of the *Idaho World* "supposed," probably with tongue in cheek, that the mode of disposing of the Yankee girls upon their arrival would be something like this:

> The ship has arrived in port. Notice has been sent to the long-haired miners, and rich bachelors of that auriferous section. The girls have been bathed by squads, platoons and brigades, in the mouth of some waterfall from the mountains; their best raiment has been put on. Standing on the poop deck, the charge d'affairs, with hair pushed back from his receding forehead, and a sharp nasal twang, thus holds forth: "Neow yeou wild beasts of this ere Pacific strand, I've brought you a whole passel of genuine ladies, right nice and fresh from Bosting, and along the shore. I have a picked lot of gals, fresh as a daisy and lively as a butterfly! I mout sell the entire lot to one man, but that would be too much of a good thing, but I'll sell you each a little charmer, warranted not to cut in the eye, big enough for the tallest miner, and small enough for the least there is among you! Walk up fellers. Stand up to the taffrail gals. No crowding on the hauser! Get eout yer dust and select yer gal!
>
> "The first I'll offer, fellers, is a freckled faced schoolmarm. Betsy Jane. The other name aint no matter. You can gin her yeourn. She is nineteen years old by the Bible, has good teeth, is twenty-seven inches around the waist, and is warranted kind in harness. How much for Betsy? Sold to Jack Longhead for five hundred dollars.
>
> "The next animile—oh! sweetheart!—fellers, is a blue-eyed Yankee gal, named Jerusha Ann. . .aint so by-ly handsome, but is heavy on the hug, and is warranted to last a life time, if she dont die first. How much for her? Come, wake up you fellers! Massachusetts wants to enlighten you!. . .Sold to Daredevil Tom for fifty ounces of dust.
>
> "Now, fellers, stand up close. Here is a stunner. Tabithia Marier, as was her Mother before her, also her Grandmother. . .eats but little—a pine gum lunch will last her a week. Sold for no fault, but Massachusetts has no further use for her, and takes this means to pay her war tax!. . .she is warranted genuine, and if not sold will be thrown ashore for you fellers to play with, and over she goes, for it is all chance you know!"[43]

"Vidette," the Washington correspondent of the *Sacramento Union*, wrote with skepticism:

> It is not probable, however, that the (more or less) fair emigrants are of the industrious order, but school marms and other ornamental rather than useful members of society who toil not neither do they spin, yet Solomon in all his glory was not arrayed like one of these.[44]

Nearer home, in Olympia, the *Washington Standard* displayed mixed feelings. "While we do not fully appreciate Mr. Mercer's motives in bringing so many really helpless people to our doors, and no families, yet we are pleased to believe they will be taken care of, if not among our own people, by our neighbors of Oregon."[45] The relief committee in Olympia, appointed to procure homes for some of these ladies, reported that eighty could be provided for there.[46] The citizens of this community had been offended at petty references to them and their neighbors, and were determined to put their best foot forward and show their maligners how wrong they were.

> We bespeak for them [the girls] a pleasant reception. They may have been deceived as to what kind of a Paradise they were approaching, but let our people greet them with kind faces and a comfortable home, until employment can be provided. Let us give the lie to the foul aspersion that the people here are a set of half-civilized barbarians. Another emigration scheme of this character should and will be promptly frowned down.[47]

That the bachelors of Vancouver, W.T., expected to benefit from this venture was evident from the curt warning they gave their friends across the Columbia river in Portland, Oregon. "If you want a shipload of girls, go and get them. There are just 39,301 yet left in Massachusetts, and if you can get a recommendation from Mr. Mercer, you can probably get some of them, but you can't have the choice of our load."[48] Ignoring this admonition, the Oregonians immediately set about making arrangements to welcome some of the girls.[49] In contrast to this, the *Alta California*, standing somewhat aloof, assumed a wait-and-see attitude.

> The only thing Mr. Mercer has to fear, so far as I can see, is that in case the girls are young and pretty, they may be snapped up by some of your wifeless young men in San Francisco. If, however, as is more than likely, they should be of the oldish maid order, they will be likely to go straight to their destinations. Californians, I judge, are not so far gone as to want any of that kind. We shall see what we shall see . . . .[50]

The British Columbians, neighbors to the north, were old hands at receiving female emigrants to their shores, since they had already greeted two parties from England.[51] The editor of the New Westminster newspaper assured the Mercer party a welcome to that community should they choose to go there.[52] From across the waters at Victoria, British Columbia, hope and enthusiasm were expressed.

> It seems that we are to be indebted to our Puget Sound friends for our next supply of the fair sex—for there is no doubt that many of the seven hundred girls now enroute from Boston will find their way across from that thinly peopled region to this city. There is therefore hope for our disconsolate bachelors.[53]

A conundrum was printed in the Seattle *Gazette*.

> A wag whose business it is to hunt breaks in the telegraph line through the woods hereabouts, and who, by the way is afflicted slightly with "gal on the brain," perpetrated the following: "Why will the Mercer party resemble the telegraph line during the coming winter? Answer: Both will want much splicing."[54]

"Let 'em sail; we are satisfied with home production," was the sally of the Jacksonville *Sentinel*,[55] to which a Washington paper, with a jibe at the so-called squaw men, promptly taunted, "You prefer 'brown sugar' do you?"[56]

The bachelors had to wait rather longer than they had originally expected, and the lonely souls filled the long empty evenings musing over the future. One even produced a poem, a parody upon Tennyson's "The Light Brigade" entitled "The Seven Hundred," and this effort, all six verses of it, was printed in the *Gazette*.[57]

The sixties being a period of intense partisanship, it was not surprising that Mercer's program was drawn into the arena of politics. During the 1865 election campaign for territorial delegate, the *Washington Democrat* charged that Mercer had gone east to recruit Negro contrabands to work in the mills.[58] This brought a vigorous denial from a mill owner, G. A. Meigs. He said, "Mr. Mercer never proposed anything of the kind to me, or any other person so far as I know, and I have not furnished him with any money or promised to do so."[59] Other papers in the territory chose sides and kept the controversy simmering until election time. Irrespective of how much weight the charges may have carried, they were not decisive. Mercer's friend, A. A. Denny, was elected.[60]

Mercer complained that "an article in the *Herald*" had criticized the purpose of the scheme and had cast aspersions upon the motives of any young woman brash enough to join. He said he felt that this article had had a disastrous effect in reducing the passenger list. Many young women wrote him, Mercer recalled,[61] enclosed the critical article, and, at the same time, canceled passage. Since searchers,[62] including this writer, have been unable to find this article in the *New York Herald*, it is possible the item may have appeared elsewhere. Many writers have mentioned the article, but they have failed to give a citation indicating the issue in which it could be found.[63]

Factors other than the *Herald* article were at work influencing the women to cancel passage. New England mills were reopening and again offering employment.[64] In the summer of 1865, a news item stated that there was a great scarcity of female operatives in New England and that wages were unprecedently high.[65] There was also a need for servant girls in Boston, and the housekeepers of that city were terrified by the rush of the girls to the factories.[66] Too, many of the women ran short of funds because of the long wait and became discouraged enough to cancel passage.

Other New York papers looked favorably upon Mercer's efforts, namely, the *Times* and the *Tribune*. The latter had this to say:

> This is the grandest and most beneficial female excursion ever inaugurated and will no doubt be very beneficial in its results. Mr. Mercer seems like a whole-souled, honest man, and has no object in view than the good of the community of which he is an honored member. And if life is spared, he can look back at three score and ten, and in almost every face of the youth, see the results of his enterprise in 1864-65. He will be the godfather of Washington Territory.[67]

Actually, it is more surprising that Mercer, instead of the girls, had not been scared out of his undertaking by what the newspapers were printing. The *Times* was somewhat amused.

> Mr. Mercer, under whose guidance and care they go, has assumed a responsibility which few men would care to lay upon themselves. . . .The venture has comic aspects which will suggest themselves, and the imagination cannot help figuring the awful task of reducing to harmony the multitudinous prejudices, caprices, and assumptions of seven hundred young ladies. Forty married men go with Mr. Mercer, and twenty young men will be his allies; but this is as a handful in contrast with the overwhelming numbers of the ladies, and might be swept into the sea in a single tempest of passion. His trust, therefore, must be in them during the voyage, as theirs in him at the end; and we believe neither will have cause for disappointment.[68]

Mercer carried with him references from Governor Pickering of Washington Territory[69] and from Massachusetts' Governor John Andrew,[70] and Edward Everett Hale, of the New England Emigrant Aid Society, was particularly active on his behalf,[71] especially in the matter of contacting prospective emigrants. Nevertheless, adversities dogged his every footstep — from the day Mercer landed in New York and found notices of President Lincoln's death posted everywhere until the hour his passengers were all safely landed at their destinations.

Mercer failed in his effort to secure the loan or services of one of the steamships that had been declared surplus at the close of the Civil War. However, the government offered to sell the S.S. *Continental* at a low appraisal cost. Mercer, lacking the necessary funds, yielded to Ben Holladay who formed the steamship company that purchased the ship and then gave Mercer a contract to transport his party to the West Coast.[72] Even after this deal was made, there were many delays in preparing the ship for the long trip. Finally, about five months after the original date set for sailing,[73] the S.S. *Continental* cleared New York harbor with only a small number of the hundreds of women whom Mercer had hoped to take west.

The Vessel

The S.S. *Continental*, a fine screw steamer of 1,626 tons measurement, was built in Philadelphia in 1862 by John Lynn, and had the following dimensions: length, 235 feet; beam, 36 feet; draft, 17 feet.[74] Her engine, built by Merrick and Sons of Philadelphia, had a cylinder of 40 inches diameter, with 50 inches stroke of piston. She had three decks and was well lighted and ventilated.[75]

> On each side are large and pleasant staterooms, which will be made as pleasant and cozy as the most fastidious young lady could desire. . .one cabin will be the exclusive sanctum of the ladies, and no gentleman will, under any circumstances, obtain admittance. A number of sewing machines will be fastened to the floor. . . .The sanitary arrangements will be fine. A large bathing room will be attached to each cabin for the use of the passengers. An inspecting committee will be appointed who will make it their business to visit all the state rooms every morning and report their condition to the doctor. A room will be fitted up expressly for the doctor where he can always be found by the sick, and it is expected he will be overwhelmed with business the first few days out. One of the rooms is. . .a library, furnished with interesting and instructive reading matter. We learn that many of our book publishers have donated some of their most valuable books to that library.[76]

> The arrangements in case of accident are complete. There are from 475 to 500 feet of hose on board which can readily be carried to any part of the ship; in case of fire, 69 buckets and 14 axes. There will be 10 large life boats, most of them metallic, and a life preserver for each passenger.[77]

One of the girls said she would venture a guess that there were staterooms for about eighty passengers, and continued, "We are all as comfortably situated as people can be on shipboard. Our food is not luxurious but quite varied and abundant. Mr. Mercer presides at the head of the table easily and gracefully."[78] She paid tribute to the ship in this fashion:

> After one month upon the ocean, one can easily understand the pride and affection which a sailor feels in his ship. My idea of the most appropriate prelude to Paradise is a voyage round the world in the *Continental*. Many times I stand at the stern of the ship and, looking along her whole length, watch her stately and graceful motion. Then she is no longer the achievement of man's hand, but a thing of life, the central heart-throbs adding to the illusion.[79]

After the war, the *Continental* was purchased from the government by the newly organized California, Oregon and Mexican Steamship Company, whose president was Ben Holladay. The price quoted was $80,000 — a fraction of the initial cost. This ship was intended to replace the *John L. Stephens* on the west-coast run to Mazatlan, Mexico.[80]

During the comparatively short life of this vessel, she seemed destined to have a precarious career. Originally built for the run between New York and Charleston, the *Continental* was requisitioned by the government during the Civil War and was used to transport troops to and from New

Orleans.[81] Then she was selected to carry Mercer's brigade to the West Coast. During the trip she was fired upon when leaving a blockaded port which she had entered by mistake. Later that same year, she again found herself in a difficult situation. "The steamer *Continental* not knowing that Corrunna occupied Mazatlan, ran into that port, when the Liberal Commander seized her with three thousand rifles and a quantity of ammunition, on the charge of being engaged in making war on Mexico."[82] She was soon extricated from this predicament. Three days after the above item appeared in the paper, the following was released: "The *Steamer Continental* brought $30,000 in treasure from Mazatlan."[83]

Unfortunately, the boat did not see long service. On September 27, 1870, she was caught in a gale and foundered while crossing the Gulf of California. Eight people lost their lives. Captain Chris Dall, in command at the time, was severely reprimanded for his conduct.[84] The *Continental*, of Mercer fame, should not be confused with a later ship of the same name which was launched at Bath, Maine, in January, 1875, and was lost in 1888.[85]

The Author

Conant was a name well known in early New England and one which has since gained wide recognition. The family history in the New World began with a Roger Conant who was identified with the founding of Salem, Massachusetts, in the early part of the seventeenth century. Nine generations and over three hundred years later,[86] another Roger Conant recorded his impressions of a singular voyage from New York to the West Coast with Asa S. Mercer and his party on the S.S. *Continental* in 1866.

Born at Waterville, Maine, in 1833[87] while his father was professor of languages and religion at Waterville College (now Colby),[88] Roger Conant was fortunate in his heritage. The scholarly and literary pursuits of both his father and his mother contributed much to the intellectual atmosphere of the family circle. Perhaps the best known of the many publications of his father, Dr. Thomas J. Conant, were the translations of the *Holy Bible* from the original Hebrew, and *Gesenius' Hebrew Grammar*.[89] Roger's mother, Hannah O'Brien Chaplin Conant, was eminent in her own right.[90] Among her numerous writings were a biography of the first missionary to Burma, Dr. A. Judson, entitled *The Earnest Man; a History of the English Bible* in 1866; and translations of many biblical tales.[91] Aside from rearing her children, four boys and six girls, and her home duties, she found time to edit the *Mother's Monthly Journal* and to contribute frequently to various periodicals.[92] She died at the family home in Brooklyn, New York, in the February preceding her son's departure for the Far West.[93]

Little is available on the early life and character of Roger Conant. A remark made later in life that as a youth he had often wished to be Gulliver may have hinted at future travels.[94] He liked the land and thought for a while of becoming a farmer, but his father preferred that he study law. Prior to 1866 when he joined the Mercer emigration to the West Coast, Conant had studied law, had served in the Union Forces during the Civil War,[95] and had been a reporter for the *New York Times*.

A comment in the *Times*, which may well have been Conant's own reporting, read:

> This voyage will be one of strange and novel interest, and it is to be hoped that some of the voyagers will give us a pen photograph in book form of the trip from New York to the Pacific Coast. Well written, it would be the most interesting sea voyage given to the public.[96]

Herein, perhaps, was expressed the germ of the idea of going west with the girls. In fact, it may have prompted the editor of his paper to send someone to chronicle the happenings en route and to select Conant, a bachelor in his early thirties, for this assignment.

An observing young man, keenly aware of the world about him, Conant created vivid word pictures of scenery, wildlife, and places visited en route. He seems to have had a talent for being in the right place at the right time, and in his journal he relates many amusing incidents involving the young ladies, the other passengers, himself, and the crew. Most of these were not included in his published reports to the *New York Times*.[97] Nor did he mention his own unsuccessful attempts to woo some of the women passengers. These romantic episodes were later recalled by Flora Pearson Engle, one of the Mercer girls.

Although the *Continental* carried the party only as far as San Francisco, the journal records the conclusion of the trip of those who secured passage on the lumber schooners, such as the barques *George Washington*, *Vidette*, *Scotland*, and *Huntsville*, and the brigs *Tanner* and *Sheet Anchor*, to Seattle and other Puget Sound ports.[98] After a brief stay in Seattle and a short excursion in Washington Territory, Mr. Conant returned on the *Caroline Reed* [99] to San Francisco where he obtained employment as a clerk and took lodgings at 135 Fifth Street.[100]

At the First Congregational Church, Conant found fellowship and an outlet for his literary talents in the Young Peoples' Social and Literary

Society.[101] As a member of the literary committee, he contributed to the society's monthly publication *Social Voices*. A version of Conant's journal, similar in content to the articles in the *Times*, was published serially in *Social Voices* during the months he was a member of its staff.[102]

Conant entertained with readings at many of the social evenings of the society. On one occasion he read an essay relating his experiences with Sherman on his march to the sea;[103] at another he recited Longfellow's "The Village Blacksmith."[104] After yet another, at which he gave a rendition entitled "Rienzi to the Romans," the critic reported:

> Mr. Conant's recitation was carefully prepared and appropriately given. The hoarseness of the speaker injured the necessarily abrupt transition near the close, and gave occasion though not excuse, for a display of ill manners among the many juveniles who rally in such numbers to the meetings of this Society.[105]

At that, he fared as well as did Miss Hancock who followed him with a vocal solo. "Miss Hancock's ballad was gracefully sung, with however, some tremulousness in the grave passages."[106] In those days a critic took his job literally and seriously.

While in San Francisco, Conant entered upon a new but apparently short-lived venture. In 1869, the following advertisement appeared in two monthly issues of the young peoples' publication and then no more.

Roger Conant	D. M. Knowlton	Jas. O'Brien
Conant	Knowlton	O'Brien

Phonographic Reporters and Copyists
604 Merchant Street (Room 10) San Francisco
Searching of Records and collections
promptly attended to.[107]

The name of Roger Conant did not appear in the *San Francisco City Directory* for 1869. It was about this time that he moved to Santa Cruz, California, a resort town on lovely Monterey Bay. There he made his home for many years. Shortly after his arrival in town, he opened an office with S. S. Roberts and their professional card read:

S. S. Roberts   R. Conant
ROBERTS AND CONANT
Attorneys and Land Agents
Land claims prosecuted to final judgment; Titles accurately searched; collections promptly made; Real Estate bought and sold; money loaned on Collateral Security.
   Agents for the Aetna Life Insurance Company. Offices in Hugo Hihn's Brick Building lately occupied by F. J. McCann, Esq.
Santa Cruz, Cal.   (My 7-tf)[108]

This advertisement continued in the *Santa Cruz Sentinel* until October, 1870, when a new professional card for Conant appeared indicating that as an attorney-at-law he had opened his own office upstairs in Baldwin's Building.[109] The next year he moved to the Courthouse, as an attorney-at-law and court commissioner.[110] Later he was a justice of the peace.[111]

Conant was very active in lodge work. At various times he served as secretary of the Odd Fellows[112] and as secretary, vice-arch, and noble-arch of Madronna Grove, No. 21, United Ancient Order of Druids.[113]

Roger Conant did not marry a Mercer girl. The *Santa Cruz Sentinel* reported his marriage on March 8, 1874, to Helen M. Hemingway of Santa Cruz, the ceremony taking place in the Congregational Church with the Reverend S. H. Willey officiating.[114] The couple thereafter lived on North Branciforte Street.[115] Mrs. Conant later became an invalid as the result of a stroke, and her husband attended her himself, carrying her onto the porch to look out on the beautiful bay on pleasant days and giving her loving care for many years.[116]

The last three years of Conant's life were spent in the Veteran's Home at Sawtelle, California (now absorbed into greater Los Angeles). He entered on August 5, 1912, and died there October 19, 1915 at the age of eighty-two. He was buried with full military honors in the Center Cemetery.[117] Among his personal effects which were sent to his relatives in the East was the manuscript of his journal, "The Cruise of the *Continental* or An Inside View of Life on the Ocean Wave."

Notes

1. *Puck, The Pacific Pictorial* (San Francisco), Vol. II, March 1, 1866, tipped in.
2. Benjamin Draper, "Dogs, Earthquakes and Emperors," *American Heritage* I (1950), 28.
3. *Sacramento Daily Union*, April 25, 1866, p. 3.
4. *Calaveras Chronicle* (Mokelumne Hill, Cal.), April 28, 1866, p. 3.
5. *Walla Walla Statesman*, September 22, 1865, p. 2.
6. *Sacramento Daily Union*, April 26, 1866, p. 3.
7. Conant, *Social Voices* (San Francisco), April 15, 1869, p. 2, hereafter referred to as *Social Voices*.
8. Harriet Stevens, Letter to the Editor, *Puget Sound Daily* (Seattle), June 2, 1866. Also reprinted in *Pacific Northwest Quarterly*, XXXV (October, 1944), 345-47. See appendix B, Document 6.
9. Clarence B. Bagley, "The Mercer Immigration," *Oregon Historical Quarterly*, V (March 1904), 24, hereafter referred to as C. B. Bagley.
10. Charles Prosch, *Reminiscences of Washington Territory* (Seattle: Prosch, 1904), p. 123, hereafter referred to as C. Prosch.
11. C. B. Bagley, p. 1; and N. M. Bogart, Reminiscences of Early Pioneer Days (Typed MS in Sophie Frye Bass Library, Seattle Historical Society, n.d.), hereafter referred to as Bogart.
12. *Washington Standard* (Olympia), December 23, 1865, p. 1.
13. Asa S. Mercer to C. B. Bagley, Mayoworth, Wyoming, November 12, 1901, C. B. Bagley, p. 12.
14. Bogart, n.p.
15. *The American Annual Cyclopedia for 1865* (New York: D. Appleton and Co., 1868), p. 533.
16. *Puget Sound Herald* (Steilacoom), October 30, 1862, p. 2.
17. C. B. Bagley, p. 1.
18. Flora Pearson Engle, "The Story of the Mercer Expedition," *Washington Historical Quarterly*, VI (October, 1915), 225-28, hereafter referred to as Engle.
19. *New York Times*, October 24, 1865, p. 5.
20. Asa S. Mercer to Governor Addison C. Gibbs, June 2, 1864, from Seattle, in letters of Governor Gibbs, Oregon Historical Society. It is doubtful if Gibbs ever responded to this letter of Mercer's. Delphine Henderson, "Asa Shinn Mercer, Northwest Publicity Agent," *Reed College Bulletin*, XXIII (January, 1945), 26.
21. C. B. Bagley, p. 23.
22. *Ibid.*, p. 22.
23. *Washington Standard* (Olympia), June 17, 1866, p. 3.
24. Harriet Stevens, *Puget Sound Daily* (Seattle), June 2, 1866.
25. C. B. Bagley, p. 15.
26. *Ibid.*, p. 23.
27. *San Francisco Examiner*, June 23, 1893, p. 15.
28. C. Prosch, pp. 123-24.
29. The headlines are taken, respectively, from the following sources: *Seattle Gazette*, November 8, 1865, p. 2; *Walla Walla Statesman*, October 29, 1865, p. 2; John Gabriel, "How Washington Got Its Women," *Evergreen Magazine*, (Seattle), I (September, 1946), 14; *New York Daily Tribune*, October 6, 1865, p. 8; *Alta California* (San Francisco), January 20, 1866, p. 1; *Ibid.; Sacramento Daily Union*, April 20, 1866, p. 2; *Vancouver Daily Post* (Victoria, B.C.), October 3, 1865, p. 3; *Mountaineer* (The Dalles, Ore.), September 6, 1865, p. 2; *New York Times*, May 22, 1866, p. 1; *Alta California* (San Francisco), January 20, 1866, p. 1.

30. *Seattle Gazette*, November 18, 1865, p. 2.
31. *Harper's Weekly Magazine*, X (January 6, 1866), 8, 9.
32. *Morning Call* (San Francisco) as quoted in *Alta California* (San Francisco), January 19, 1866, p. 1.
33. *New York Times*, October 2, 1865, p. 4.
34. *Springfield Republican* as quoted in *Alta California* (San Francisco), January 28, 1866, p. 1.
35. *New York Times*, September 30, 1865, p. 8.
36. *Commonwealth* (Boston), May 12, 1866, p. 3.
37. *Ibid.*, December 16, 1865, p. 3.
38. *Ibid.*, November 18, 1865, p. 3.
39. *Ibid.*, July 22, 1865, p. 3.
40. *Alta California* (San Francisco), February 4, 1866, p. 1.
41. *Walla Walla Statesman*, October 29, 1865, p. 2.
42. *La Crosse Democrat* (Wisconsin), as quoted in *Walla Walla Statesman, ibid.*
43. *Idaho World* (Idaho City), October 28, 1865, p. 1.
44. *Sacramento Daily Union* as quoted by *Pacific Tribune* (Olympia), September 23, 1865, p. 2.
45. *Washington Standard* (Olympia), October 14, 1865, p. 2.
46. *Morning Oregonian* (Portland, Ore.), October 17, 1865, p. 1.
47. *Pacific Tribune* (Olympia), April 28, 1866, p. 2.
48. *Vancouver Register* (Washington), October 21, 1865, p. 2.
49. *Morning Oregonian* (Portland, Ore.), October 6, 1865, p. 3.
50. *Alta California* (San Francisco), September 8, 1865, p. 1.
51. *Colonist* (Victoria, B.C.), September 29, 1862, and *ibid.*, January 12, 1863.
52. *The British Columbian* (New Westminster, B.C.), September 30, 1865, p. 3.
53. *Vancouver Daily Post* (Victoria, B.C.), September 28, 1865, p. 3.
54. *Seattle Gazette*, October 28, 1865, p. 2.
55. *Oregon Sentinel* (Jacksonville), February 10, 1866, p. 2.
56. *Washington Standard* (Olympia), February 24, 1866, p. 2.
57. *Seattle Gazette*, November 18, 1865, p. 1.
58. *Washington Democrat* (Olympia), May 13, 1865, p. 2.
59. *Ibid.*, May 20, 1865, p. 2.
60. C. B. Bagley, p. 23.
61. *Ibid.*
62. Murray Morgan, *Skid Road* (New York: Viking Press, 1951), p. 64 footnote.
63. Stewart Holbrook, *A Yankee Exodus* (New York: Macmillan Co., 1950), p. 247; Archie Binns, *Northwest Gateway* (Garden City, N.Y.: Doubleday Doran and Co., 1941), p. 190; E. B. Meany, *History of the State of Washington* (New York: Macmillan Co., 1910), p. 262.
64. *New York Times*, August 30, 1865, p. 5.
65. *Boston Evening Courier*, July 27, 1865, p. 1.
66. *New York Times*, October 27, 1865, p. 4.
67. *New York Daily Tribune*, October 6, 1865, p. 8.
68. *New York Times*, October 2, 1865, p. 4.
69. *Ibid.*, September 30, 1865, p. 8.
70. *The American Annual Cyclopedia for 1865*, p. 533.
71. Edward Everett Hale to Frank B. Cooper dated Roxbury, Mass., November 16, 1903. See appendix B, Document 5.
72. C. B. Bagley, p. 23.

73. *Idaho World* (Idaho City), September 9, 1865, p. 1. Herein the date August 20 was listed as the first date set for the *Continental* sailing.

74. *American Lloyd's Registry of American and Foreign Shipping* (New York: T. D. Taylor, R. T. Hartshorne and J. F. H. King, compilers, 1879), No. 159, p. 9 of "Steamers."

75. *New York Times*, October 2, 1865, p. 8.

76. *Seattle Gazette*, February 2, 1866, p. 2.

77. *New York Times*, December 4, 1865, p. 8.

78. Harriet Stevens, "A Journal of Life on the Steamer *Continental*," *Puget Sound Daily* (Seattle), June 6, 1866, p. 2.

79. *Ibid.*, May 31, 1866, p. 3.

80. *Puget Sound Daily* (Seattle), April 26, 1865, p. 2.

81. *New York Times*, December 4, 1865, p. 8.

82. *Ibid.*, September 26, 1866, p. 5.

83. *Ibid.*, September 29, 1866, p. 4.

84. *Lewis' and Dryden's Marine History of the Pacific Northwest*, Edgar Wilson Wright, ed. (Portland: Lewis and Dryden, 1895), p. 189.

85. F. C. Matthews, *American Merchant Ships 1850-1890* (Salem, Mass.: Marine Research Society, 1930), pp. 84-86.

86. *Dictionary of American Biography* (New York: Charles Scribner & Sons, 1930), p. 337.

87. F. J. Carey, director Domiciliary Service, Veterans Administration Center, Los Angeles, to Lenna Deutsch, March 7, 1956.

88. *Social Voices*, March 21, 1867, p. 4.

89. *New Century Cyclopedia of Names* (New York: Appleton, Century, Crofts, 1954), p. 1,051; and *New York Times*, August 11, 1865, p. 5.

90. *Dictionary of American Biography*, p. 337.

91. S. Austin Allibone, *Dictionary of Authors-Supplement* (Philadelphia: J. B. Lippincott, 1896), I, 372.

92. *American Annual Cyclopedia for 1865*, p. 167.

93. *New York Times*, January 4, 1866, p. 8.

94. *Santa Cruz Sentinel*, February 4, 1871, p. 2.

95. Carey to Deutsch, March 7, 1956.

96. *New York Times*, October 2, 1865, p. 8.

97. *Ibid.*, April 22, 1866, p. 5.; *ibid.*, May 6, 1866, p. 1; *ibid.*, June 10, 1866, p. 1; and *ibid.*, December 10, 1866, p. 2.

98. *Puget Sound Weekly* (Seattle), May 14, 1866, p. 6.

99. *Social Voices*, April 15, 1869, p. 2.

100. *San Francisco Directory* (San Francisco: H. G. Langley, 1868) p. 150.

101. *Social Voices*, April 16, 1869, p. 2.

102. The first episode in the serial version began with the issue of November 21, 1867; the final eipsode appeared in April, 1869.

103. *Social Voices*, August 20, 1868, p. 6.

104. *Ibid.*, March 18, 1869, p. 5.

105. *Ibid.*, September 17, 1868, p. 6.

106. *Ibid.*, March 18, 1869, p. 5.

107. *Ibid.*, February 18, 1869, p. 6; and *ibid.*, March 18, 1869, p. 6.

108. *Santa Cruz Sentinel*, May 14, 1870, p. 1.

109. *Ibid.*, October 22, 1870, p. 1.

110. *Ibid.*, November 11, 1878, p. 1, intermittently until May 23, 1879, p. 1.

111. *Classified Business Directory for Santa Cruz, E. Santa Cruz, Watsonville, &c.* (San Francisco: California Directory Co., 1904-5), p. 45.
112. *Santa Cruz Sentinel,* July 18, 1874, p. 3.
113. *Ibid.,* December 3, 1874, p. 3; *ibid.,* May 2, 1874, p. 2; and *ibid.,* November 7, 1874, p. 2.
114. *Ibid.,* March 14, 1874, p. 2.
115. *Thurston's Business and Resident Directory 1912-1913* (Santa Cruz, California: Howe's, *ca.* 1911), p. 57.
116. Mrs. Helen Loud Poland, niece of Roger Conant, in personal interview with Lenna Deutsch, July, 1954.
117. Carey to Deutsch, March 7, 1956.

THE CRUISE
OF THE CONTINENTAL

OR

*An Inside View of a Life
On the Ocean Wave*

❋❋❋❋❋❋❋❋❋❋❋❋❋❋❋❋❋❋❋❋❋❋❋

ROGER CONANT'S JOURNAL

Left New York Jan. 16th, 1866
Arrived in San Francisco April 24th, 1866

1

A BELATED DEPARTURE

THE ADVERTISEMENT published throughout the country by one Mercer,[1] calling himself a Female Emigrant Agent from Washington Territory, [saying] that he would take 700 single women to Washington Territory free of charge and give them immediate employment as soon as they landed on [the] shores of Puget Sound, naturally excited in the public mind an inquiry, as to what all this meant? A natural distrust as to the man's intentions seemed to prevail. It was hard to believe that any man, specially a young man, would be so philanthropic as to be willing to spend his entire fortune in an operation where he could receive no benefit.

He was looked upon as an adventurer, and many efforts were put forth to prevent the expedition from becoming a success. (These efforts proved so far successful that only 100 women,[2] a majority of them widows, finally consented to place themselves under the charge and guidance of a man whom they had never heard of before.) It was a bold act on their part, and brought down upon their heads the derision of the entire community. They were called husband hunters, and hints as to their character flew as thick and fast as snowflakes. Most of them were from the middle class of New England society and were respectable well meaning people, and their conduct during the voyage would have called forth strong expressions of praise from their stern old Puritan ancestors. I propose to give a faithful chronicle of everything that transpired on ship board, from the time we left New York until the separation and settlement of the party on the Pacific Coast.

In giving a faithful account of all that transpired on the good ship *Continental* during her voyage from New York to San Francisco, we shall often be obliged to tread on some body's corns. We hope that they will submit to the inconvenience good naturedly and if they must retaliate will use only their tongues.

[Tuesday,] Jan. 16th. Today having been finally settled upon for the sailing of the *Continental*, we were early at Mr. Mercer's office, 91 West St., and learned that the ship would probably sail about 11 o'clock that morning. Wishing to see what effect the good news would have upon the fair virgins, we made our way up to Lovejoy's Hotel where a large party of them had for some days been sojourning till the time should arrive for them to go on board. We found them in fine spirits. The near prospect of sailing seemed to perfectly electrify them. Instead of cold dark and contracted brows that made one think as he went among them that he was passing through the North west passage, their faces were wreathed with smiles, and their eyes fairly sparkled with delight.[3] Our entrance into the parlor was greeted with a hundred questions such as women only know how to ask. "When is the steamer going to sail?" "Are our hotel bills paid yet?" "Are you sure that we shall leave this hateful place to day?" came thick and fast as snow flakes. In utter bewilderment we could only say,[4] "Yes! Yes!! Everything is all right, get all your things together at once." In an instant everything was in the greatest confusion. Porters flew up stairs and down followed by the excited ladies who took them by the button hole and pulled them in all sorts of directions, seeming determined that their particular trunks and band boxes should be the first on the express wagon. At last the final act was brought to a close by the safe stowing away of the last lady in the coach, and the curtain fell over the scene. At 3 p.m. the noble ship left her berth at pier 2 N.R. [North River] and sweeping proudly into the stream sailed slowly down the bay.

For some days before the Expedition sailed it was well known that Mr. Mercer's bank account had failed. In plain language, the whole affair promised to become a grand failure, and the prospect of the girls' ever reaching the virgin soil of Washington Territory was exceedingly dubious. At this critical moment when it seemed as if all his grand schemes were doomed to vanish into air, a luckless wight, who is known to California newspaper readers as Sniktaw,[5] sailed right into his clutches. He, Sniktaw, was permitted to spend the best part of his life in the mountains, from which the Devil had at an early day been ordered to depart. Thus dwelling in a pure atmosphere away from the temptations of the world, honest Sniktaw lived

on year after year, laying up his honest gains earned by hard labor with
the pick and shovel, and boiling his pork and beans over his little camp
fire, utterly unconscious of the many devils roaming in the valleys below.
But unfortunately for Sniktaw he was seized with a strong desire to see
the world and leaving his safe mountain retreat set forth upon his travels.
While in New York, visiting the lions and wondering as to the best means
of investing his little capital, his eye lit upon one of Mercer's advertise-
ments. A grand idea at once flashed across the vision of Sniktaw. Here was
an opportunity to make a pile of money without labor. Taking the advertisement in one hand, he sat down, and resting his head upon the other,
and, leaning his elbow upon the table, reasoned thus to himself. "Here
are seven hundred virgins[6] going to a country inhabited only by men. Of
course there will be a great demand for wives, and the men in order to
be married must be dressed. Why cannot I provide them with the clothes?"
Full of this idea he rushed down to Mercer's office and asked the latter
if he was an honest man. Of course Mercer told him that there was no
man living who was so near Mt. Zion as himself, and produced the recommendation of Gov. Pickering, a bigger rascal than himself, as proof. This
was enough for Sniktaw, and he handed over $8,000 to an utter stranger
and telling him to buy that amount of wedding suits promised him 10 per
cent of the sales. Mercer took the money, paid the passage of the virgins
to the Territory and bought the goods on credit, his victim never once sus-
pecting that there was anything out of the way.[7] And thus it was that the
expedition succeeded in leaving New York.

Soon after getting under way a rumor began to float round the ship
that there were some persons on board whose passage had not been paid
for. No one seemed to know who would be so unfortunate as to draw a
blank. Expectation was on tiptoe, and the poor people gathered together
in little groups talking it over and wondering if they were among those
who would be singled out and sent back. At last the steamer came to anchor off quarantine, Staten Island,[8] and the passengers having all been sent
into the lower saloon were called up one by one and their tickets exam-
ined. Two men with their families and sixteen virgins were selected for
a return voyage to New York and were ordered to get their things together
and go on board the tug boat then lying long side. May we never look upon
such a scene again.[9] Disappointed virgins, before whose sparkling eyes had
danced a pair of pantaloons for many weeks, wept aloud at the dismal prospect before them and vowed that they would tear Mercer's eyes out before
they would go back. Others, more strong minded, locked themselves up

in the state rooms and dared the officers to break open the door and remove them.[10] One gray haired old man told a pitiful story. Said he, "I gave
up my business at a great sacrifice and have come many hundred miles
upon the assurance of that man that I could do better in a new country.
He told me to come at once as the ship would sail in a few days. I have
spent all my money for the board of my family and here I am, a stranger,
going to be sent back to New York on this bitter cold night with a wife
and five children where I have neither a roof to shelter them nor a cent
to buy them a loaf of bread," and the strong man bowed his head upon
his breast and wept.[11] And where was the man, who had caused so much
misery, all this time? The disappointed virgins screamed, "Mr. Mercer!
Mr. Mercer!!" The gray haired man hoarsely shouted, "Mr. Mercer! Mr.
Mercer!!" But no Mr. Mercer answered their appeals, and a thorough search
of all the state rooms failed to discover his place of concealment. Some
one said that he had been arrested for boarding house debts in New York
and was in the lock up. At this announcement there was great confusion
among the virgins, and some of them coming to us, said, "Mr. Conant,
if the ship sails without Mr. Mercer we shall look to you for protection."
Thoroughly appalled at the prospect before us, we secretly formed a plan
to run away from the ship the first night she reached San Francisco.

Among those selected by Mercer to be sent back were two young orphan girls who had placed themselves under his protection. With cold in-
difference and perfect heartlessness he was going to send these young girls
back. And what must have been their fate thrown as they would have been
upon the cold charities of the world without a friend and without a dollar.
Pitying their utterly helpless condition Miss Mary Bermingham interceded
for them with her brother, and he gave them their passage to San Francisco. But where was Mr. Mercer all this time? The steam tug had left
for the city, carrying the disappointed virgins whose high expectations of
casting the sun light of their presence over the lonely hearth stone of some
back woodman's cabin among the forests of Washington Territory, were so
suddenly blasted, and the gray haired man with his family with them. Everything was quiet. The virgins now that all danger was past had recovered
their equinimity, and had even forgotten their less fortunate associates. A
bright smile now overspread the face of a young and interesting looking
virgin as she passed into the lower saloon, and requested two of the men
to remove the hatches from one of the coal holes. There was at once great
excitement among the virgins and all gathered round, anxious to see what
was going to happen. The young virgin then looking down into the hole,

called out, "They are all gone now, Mr. Mercer; you can come out." A heavy lumbering tread from below heralded the approach of the great benefactor of the virgin race. Soon a shock of red hair deeply besprinkled with coal dust, bearing a strong resemblance to a zebra's skin, appeared below the opening. Then a pair of red eyes lifted themselves to the light. And soon a pair of hands were thrown upward in an appealing manner. He was seized by two strong men and was soon landed on the floor of the saloon. He was at once surrounded by the virgins and, Richard was himself again.[12] Some of them, disgusted at his want of pluck, refused to speak to him. Some were too glad to see him, and were willing to overlook the weak point which he had exhibited, in not telling these people that they could not go, but allowed them to come on board, and then leaving the dirty work for others to perform.

Wed., Jan. 17th. The extreme cold last night drove the virgins early to their state rooms, but they were up bright and early this morning running about the decks, laughing, chattering and having a high time generally. Oh! they were so glad that they were out of that hateful dirty old New York. And they all hoped that it would be a long time before they should again see this side of the Continent. At 7 o'clock the gong was sounded and the virgins rushed down to what they declared to be the first real good meal that they had enjoyed for weeks. At 9 a.m. we took anchor and went to sea.

Casting Up Their Accounts

A change now came over the dreams of the fair passengers. The bright rosy cheeks which had greeted us on all sides began to assume an ashy hue, and the smiling cheerful faces changed to those of deep resignation, till at last (must the sad tale be told), with Jonah like submission they tightly clasped the railing of the ship, and with outstretched necks commenced casting up their accounts with old Father Neptune.[13] This state of things could not last long, and before sundown all but four of them were tenderly laid away in their berths.

A Rough Night

Thurs., Jan. 18th. Last night, our first at sea, was anything but pleasant or agreeable. There was a chopping wind round to the westward and freshening up. A heavy cross sea from S.W. and N.W. made the ship roll fearfully. Dishes and furniture seemed to be seized with the contagion, and rolled and rattled about making clatter enough to frighten most of the virgins completely out of their senses. Some half dozen suddenly wakened from sleep by the dreadful racket, thought that the ship was certainly going to the bottom, and that Mr. Mercer was the only man who could save them from such a direful fate. With frantic haste they rushed to his state room and commenced a tongue assault most fearful to hear. "Oh, Mr. Mercer, get up! get up!! Oh, Mr. Mercer, if you don't get up we shall all be drowned!!" fell upon the ears of that most unfortunate of men, who, while hastily drawing on his pants, probably called to mind those beautiful lines:

"Oh, where shall rest be found!
Rest for the weary soul!"

He was soon among them and demanded in a stern voice, who gave them permission to disturb his rest?[14] The virgins gave him a half frightened look, and then fled in dismay to their state rooms. A young virgin had a presentiment that something was wrong with the ship, and that it was her mission to find out what was the matter. Stepping from her state room, she looked in direction of the stern of the ship, when suddenly she received a jet of water, which was pouring in through one of the port holes, that had not been securely fastened, directly in one of her eyes. A dreadful suspicion at once flashed across her mind. Yes, it must be so! The whole end of the ship was stove in, and it was her mission to inform the Captain of the dreadful fate that was impending over him and his fair cargo. She seemed as if possessed with wings as she flew rapidly down the saloon, up the stairs, and opening the door of the upper cabin on the port side, was thrown violently into the arms of the *Times* man.[15] It was fortunate for both that at the moment the ship gave a roll starboard for otherwise he would [be] gone to sea with a mermaid. Throwing his arm round her waist, he pulled her into the saloon and shut the door. She was a sensible New England virgin and showed no signs of going off into a fit of hysterics, but looked upon the whole affair as a good joke. The port hole was soon secured, and her mind relieved.

Guided by certain doleful sounds one of the gentlemen opened a state room door and found a virgin weeping bitterly and sighing deeply. The moment she caught sight of him, she threw out her arms towards him and exclaimed, "Oh, Sir! cannot you put me ashore at New York in a row boat?" The gale being at its height, and the distance to New York over one hundred miles he respectfully declined the delightful honor, and advising her not to make a fool of herself but to go to sleep, he left her to her private griefs. It continued to blow very hard all night. Some very heavy seas were shipped, breaking adrift some of the boats and it was with the greatest difficulty that they were finally secured. On account of the extraordinary rolling, they were obliged during the night to change the heading of the ship. This morning the rolling became easier and they succeeded in keeping her on her course.

Sat., Jan. 20th. During the past three days our time has been entirely occupied in taking care of the sea sick virgins. Let us pass over in silent respect the many scenes which we were obliged to pass through, for no one who has not enjoyed the experience can appreciate them. Yesterday while holding the head of a young virgin, the ship gave a sudden lurch. In order to save our self, we grasped at some thing, we knew not at the moment what, and lo! it was the waist of the unfortunate virgin. In another second we were lying on the opposite side of the state room, with her in our arms. As she was in her night dress, her feelings must have been anything but pleasant. We looked at each other for half a minute, inexpressible astonishment depicted in our faces. We were called to a realizing sense of our situation, by a young lady from an upper berth, exclaiming "You great Muggins why don't you put her back in the berth?" This afternoon while walking the port side of the ship, a young and interesting virgin suddenly exclaimed "Oh, Mr. Conant!" We at once rushed to her side and tenderly inquired as to the state of her health. She said nothing, but placed her hands across her stomach in an impressive manner. We instantly seized her by the arm pits, and hurrying her to the railing, held her there while she cast her bread upon the waters. Shortly after, Mr. Mercer came to us and said "I wish that you would go down and ask Miss Stiles [Staples] if she would not like to come up on deck. She has been very sick and needs the fresh air." We at once went below and peeped into the state room door. As our shadow darkened the passage way, a tall, dark visaged, sour grained looking virgin, aged—the Lord knows what,—she must certainly have been born before the flood, turned round and growled out "What do you want?" In our blandest manner we replied that we had come down to see if she would not like to go on deck and enjoy a little fresh air. "No I wouldn't," she replied, "clear out," and we cleared out, inwardly thanking her for the answer. While going down [to] the saloon, one of the state room doors flew violently open, and a very sea sick virgin was thrown from her berth directly across our path. "This is rather an abrupt introduction," we said in a sympathizing voice, "and is what may be called the free and easy style, but if you have no objection we will assist you to your berth." She made no reply, but springing to her feet like a kitten rushed into her state room and slammed the door after her. A low moan now reaches our ear from a state room on the opposite side of the saloon and we find one of the little school marms just recovering from her sea sickness. "Oh, Mr. Conant," she exclaimed, "the air is so close, I shall suffocate if I remain here!" "You had better let me assist you on deck," we replied, "where you will have plenty of fresh air." She held out her hands to be assisted to rise, but the poor child was too weak to walk, so we took her in our arms and carried her on deck. She was very sensible and did not scream or go into hysterics. On reaching the deck we placed her in a chair, sat down by her side and told her to lay her head on our shoulder, and there she sat and enjoyed herself like a sensible virgin, all the afternoon.

We do not know whether the sentiment

"Oh, for a lodge in some vast widder's nest!"[16]

ever entered in and took possession of Mr. Mercer's soul. Or whether in his innocence and child like simplicity, he ever contemplated making a charge upon such a citidel. But his actions today give rise to a strong suspicion, that he has at least some inclination in that direction. The sea was very heavy, and the good ship rolled about with a careless freedom, as if utterly regardless of the feelings of the poor land birds, whose sea legs were yet so weak as to compel them to dance the fantastic toe in a manner decidedly more amusing than agreeable. The agent of the Female Emigration Expedition to Washington Territory was sitting in the main saloon, on a three legged stool, gravely watching the actions of some of the ladies on the sofa opposite. Suddenly as if acting in concert with his feelings, the ship gave a heavy lurch, taking the stool from under his legs, and sending the unfortunate gentleman, with a rapidity of motion over which he had no control to the opposite side, where in a most unlover like manner, he blushingly laid his head upon the bosom of a young and buxom widow. He has not yet divulged his feelings upon the subject, but judging from his unusually grave and subdued manner, it must have been a dreadful shock to his nervous system.

Before proceeding further with our Journal we will give some account of the officers, and the passengers,[17] as some of them will occupy a conspicuous place in these pages.

Capt. Winser, the Captain, is a tall fine looking elderly gentleman. He has a strong well knit frame, fine gray hair, and keen gray eyes. He is a thorough seaman and a strict disciplinarian when on duty. He was for a long time in the U.S. Navy and was regarded by the Government as one of the best officers in the service. In the treatment of his passengers, he is dignified, gentle and considerate, and all the virgins seem to enter-tain the greatest respect for him. He seems always to be on the alert to correct and to prevent the many petty little annoyances which are always to be encountered in so long a voyage. He is accompanied by his wife and daughter. Mrs. Winser is a very pleasant lady, gentle and quiet in her man-ners, yet always ready to do everything in her power to make the voyage pleasant to the virgins. Miss Minnie Winser is a very fine young lady just turned 17. She is lively and full of fun from morning till night. She is a great favorite with everybody. Miss Mary Bermingham and her sister, Miss Bessie Bermingham, are going to San Francisco as guests of the com-pany to which the steamer belongs. Their brother Capt. Bermingham is the company's agent in San Francisco. They are both very intelligent and accomplished ladies, easy and graceful in their manners, and always ready and willing to do their part towards making the voyage a pleasant one. Their society is becoming a necessity to us.

The Chief Officer is a German by birth, and appears to be a very well educated and intelligent man. Yet one can see from all his actions that he is very much inclined to be tryanical and overbearing in his manners, not only to the men who are under him but also to the passengers; the elder virgins coming under his particular spite.

Peter McDougall, the 2d Mate, is a jolly old tar who has sailed the seas for 30 years. He is very gentle in his treatment of the virgins, and is the best liked man on ship board.

Messrs. Tennant & Rowland, the Engineers, seem to be very gentle-manly young men. They were selected for their present position on ac-count of the high standing which they held in the profession. The Engine is always kept in fine working order, and everything connected with the department is in a neat and orderly condition.

Washington Debro, the purser, is a gentlemanly young fellow, and ap-pears not only willing but anxious to wait upon the younger virgins, for whose society he has shown a decided predilection. Mrs. Hanna & her little boy, Mr. & Mrs. Ralston, who live at Rio de Janiero and are on their way home, are the only passengers who do not belong to what is termed the Mercer party. Of the members of that party we have only space to men-tion a few who took an active part in everything that transpired on ship board. Mrs. A. D. Chase is a widow lady of a very independent turn of mind and is always ready to free her mind upon any subject that she thinks requires her attention. She is particularly down on Mercer, and is a regu-lar thorn in that gentleman's side. She is a clairvoyant physician, and is

blest with what is called the second sight. She predicts for Mercer anything but a promising future. Mrs. Hanna has given her the title of "Sallie
Brass." Miss B_____ L_____ is a very nice lady always smiling and pleasant and ready to help any one in trouble. She is blest with a remarkable
appetite, and although she sits at the first table is able to sit through the
second, and is the last one to leave it. Some of the girls have given her
the title of "Soup Destroyer."[18]

Miss H_____ is a don't care a snap for anybody sort of character.
Her manner and style of conversation are coarse and uncultivated. She can
swear like a private and don't object to a good glass of wine when she can
get it. Hearing her say that she had read a good bit, we questioned her
as to the character of the books she had read. She replied that she didn't
know nothin about the poets or them things, but the best book she ever
read was "Doe Sticks' High Life in New York."

Mr. McDougal has given her the title of "Pontoon."

Miss A_____ G_____ is one of the most remarkable characters that
ever came under our observation. Her mind is remarkably well stored with
knowledge, but is not sufficiently well balanced to give it a practical turn.
Two months before the Expedition sailed she wrote to Gov. Pickering, and
requested, as a particular favor, that she might be known as "The Old Maid
of the Territory" which request was granted. Mr. McDougal has given her
the title of "Mother Carey's Chicken." We will describe the other characters as we have occasion to bring them in.[19]

Sun., Jan. 21st. This is our first Sunday at sea. The morning dawned
clear and cold. As we stood on the upper deck this morning our thoughts
went back to the dear home circle in Brooklyn; of the little brother who
was lying on a bed of sickness and pain, from which perhaps he never would
rise.[20] And we almost regretted the step that took us away from his side.
But away with such thoughts. He is in God's hands and he will do with
him what seemeth him best. There goes the gong, I wonder what's up?
There comes Jimmy Lord, perhaps he can enlighten me on the subject.
"Mr. Mercer is going to have service in the upper saloon and wishes that
you would come and help sing." The good Lord protect us! Mr. Mercer
preach! How dare the man profane the name of his maker by attempting
to teach others what he needs so much to learn himself? We are obliged
to pass Miss Mary Bermingham's door on our way to the saloon where
the services are to be held, and we ask her if she is going to hear Mr. Mercer
preach? "No, Mr. Conant," she replied, "I think that Mr. Mercer is a hypo-
crite and my conscience would smite me if I should encourage him in such

work for others to perform.

Jan. 17th — The extreme cold last night drove the virgins early to their state rooms, but they were up bright and early this morning running about the decks, laughing chattering and having a high time generally. Oh! they were so glad that they were out of that hateful dirty old New York, And they all hoped that it would be a long time before they should again see this side of the Continent. At 7 oclock the gong was sounded, and the virgins rushed down to what they declared to be the first real good meal that they had enjoyed for 1 week. At 9 a.m. we took anchor and went to sea

Casting Up Their Accounts.

A change now came over the dreams of the fair passengers. The bright rosy cheeks which had greeted us on all sides began to assume an ashy hue, and the smiling cheerful faces change to those of deep resignation, till at last (must the the sad tale be told) with Jonah like submission they tightly clasped the railing of the ship, and with our stretched necks commenced casting up their accounts with old Father Neptune

This state of things could not last long, and before sundown all but four of them were tenderly laid away in their berths.

A Rough Night.

Jan. 18th — Last night, our first at sea, was any thing but pleasant or agreeable. There was a chopping wind round to the westward and freshening up. A heavy cross sea from S.W. and N.W. made the ship roll fearfully. Dishes and furniture seemed to be seized with the contagion, and rolled and rattled about making clatter enough to frighten most of the virgins completely out of their senses. Some half dozen suddenly wakened from sleep by the dreadful racket,

A page from Roger Conant's Journal

Seattle W.S.
June 2d 1864

Gov. Gibbs
Portland
Ogn.

Dear Sir:

Feeling a deep interest in the education of the youth of this new region, and knowing that you are no less interested, I write you asking that you cooperate with me in inducing New England teachers to come among us for the purpose of establishing good schools.

I first arrived here with eleven young ladies from Massachusetts, practical teachers, and next winter contemplate visiting the east again for a similar purpose. Oregon needs many teachers. Ascertain how many you can dispose of, and by your assisting me

in the way of traveling expenses, I will escort as many teachers from the east as you may wish.

If you can work with me in this enterprise, please address me at Seattle W.S.

Yours
Respectfully
A.C. Mercer

A letter from Asa Mercer to Governor Gibbs of Oregon
(Oregon Historical Society)

a course." She is right! Never the less we shall go in and see what he has got to say. After singing a hymn, he made a prayer, and then picked a copy of the *Independent* out of his pocket and read one of Mr. Beecher's sermons.[21] He at least showed his common sense in not trying to compose one him self. Of all the members of the party there was only one who ever said anything about making a martyr of him self by going out to raise the moral tone of society in the Territory. A few days before the expedition sailed an old man came into Mercer's office, and made many inquiries respecting the state of religious feeling in the country,–the number of Churches &c. stating that he did not wish to go where he could not enjoy the highest religious privileges. Although not entirely satisfied with the answers he received he obtained some tickets at the same time remarking that on reaching the Territory he should make it his business to go about doing good. There are some parties on board, who came from the same place, and appear to be well acquainted with his former history. And their ventilation of it must prove anything but pleasant to the aged sinner. This amorous youth, whose hoary head and trembling footsteps show him to be tottering on the borders of the grave, deserted his wife and eight children and commenced a new voyage on the sea of life with a young and buxom Irish lass whom he calls his wife. This promising couple are accompanied by a promising youth aged 6 months, who they call Jimmy Lincoln. Some of the girls have given him the sobriquet of *"Old High Daddy."* This morning, Mr. Mercer read the 5th chapter of Matthew, little dreaming that the old sinner was standing behind him tossing his unfortunate off spring up and down in the most violent manner, as if wishing to impress upon the minds of all present, that there was at least one practical illustration of the passage on hand.

Monday, Jan. 22d. Here comes Mother Carey's Chicken. She seems to skim instead of walk over the deck. I make way for her and she sits down by my side, and in her quick impetuous way at once commences the conversation.

Mother Carey's Chicken: "Don't you think Mr. Conant that it is a perfect shame for all these children to waste all these valuable days in idleness?"

Mr. C.: "I do indeed. If some lady who is going out as a teacher would start a little school a great deal of good might be accomplished."

Mother Carey's Chicken: "I will go and see the Captain about it right away." And off started the little woman on her mission. Behold then a little school started this very afternoon in one of the life boats, on the hurricane deck, composed of ten little boys and girls hard at work, studying geography, reading, writing, arithmetic &c and in the midst of all sat the little school marm, helping this one and that over a hard place. Some of these boys and girls when looking back over their early life, may lay all their after success in life[22] to Mother Carey's Chicken's little school in the life boat on board the *Continental*.

While seated in our state room last night we over heard the following conversation between the Miss Berminghams' of which one, Roger Conant, was the subject:

Miss Bessie: "I think that Mr. Conant is a regular old fool."

Miss Mary: "He seems to be a very nice quiet young man."

Miss Bessie: "Yes, but then he is always hanging round that great coarse Miss _____. How he can fancy her is entirely beyond my comprehension."

Miss Mary: "It is nothing more than a passing fancy and will soon wear away. I suppose he thinks that he might as well flirt with her as with any one else."

Miss Bessie: in a quick, impetuous voice, "Well I don't admire his taste any how."

It opened my eyes not a little, men are always such consummate fools upon such matters that the overhearing of the conversation of two lady friends upon his merits and short comings does not injure him in the least provided he receives it with a becoming spirit.

Tuesday, Jan. 23rd. The piano which has had full sway of the fore part of the upper saloon, was set upon its legs this morning much to the relief of some of the anxious Mothers and more particularly to the old Doctor,[23] who yesterday received a severe shock of the bowels, which proved not at all pleasant to a man of his sensitive organization. He was making an eloquent speech to some of the ladies, when the steamer gave one of those unfortunate lurches for which she is celebrated, and prostrated the Dr. full length over the piano. It was not known at first which was most injured by the collision. But as the Doctor soon recovered, while the piano was out of tune for the rest of the voyage, I concluded that of the two, the Doctor's stomach had proved the strongest. We have music now from the rising of the sun to the going down thereof. The only accomplished performer on board is Mrs. Ralston,[24] who is very obliging and seldom refuses a request to play. Miss Ida Barlow is a fair player and is a very good singer. She is thorn no. 2 in poor old Mercer's side. Mrs. Boardman, a blind lady, sings and plays very sweetly. She is a remarkable character and can learn a piece of music quicker than one blest with sight. Her husband will sit by her side and tell her the notes, and she will strike the notes on the piano while he pronounces them to her. After going over the piece two or three times, she can play it with as much rapidity as if she saw the notes. Her husband is a tall disjointed Yankee,—tow headed and standing six feet in his stockings. He is as thin as a bean pole and seldom visits the wash tub. It is a blessed thing that she cannot see, for if she should obtain one glance of her husband, she would certainly sue for divorce. He is very devoted to his little blind wife, and his kindness makes up for many other defects. He has received the sobriquet of *"Slim Jim."*

Friday, Jan. 26th. The virgins have recovered from their sea sickness and are becoming accustomed to the rolling of the ship. The[y] swarm every part of it like a hive of bees, and are getting to be on pretty intimate terms with the young officers. One of them, young, pretty and smart, has taken a strong fancy to the 3d Engineer, who seems nothing loath to the close attentions which he receives. The day after her sickness the young lady asked Mr. G_____ if he would not be kind enough to give her a glass of water as she felt rather faint. He at once brought it to her, and at the same time asked her if she would not like a doughnut and a pickle as they had some very nice ones in the mess room. "Oh, Sir!" she replied, "I would indeed, for they must taste real refreshing after the fare we receive."[25] Mr. Mercer went up to her a few minutes ago and requested her to walk into his state room as he wanted to have a little conversation with her. They are together now, and as we happen to know his opinion of the officers, it is our opinion that he is giving her a little advise as to her future treatment of them.

This morning Mr. Mercer brought out great skeins of yarn, and the ladies, after making the men hold them while they wound them into balls, commenced knitting as if all their future happiness depended upon their finishing the socks at once. "Miss A_____" said we, to a bright and pretty virgin, "what are you knitting all these socks for?" "Oh!" said she, "Mr. Mercer is going to hold a great fair when we get to Seattle, and these socks are to be sold to pay him for his expense and trouble in bringing us." "Well," said we, "if the bachelors of that country do not succeed in getting a wife, they will have something to keep their toes warm." Miss A_____ "Oh, we are going to make up a whole lot of shirts too."[26]

Mr. C_____ "Yes,—well that looks rather suspicious. Do you intend to get married, Miss A_____ when you reach the Territory?"

Miss A_____ "I did not come out for that purpose but if I receive a good offer, I shall take the matter into consideration."

This afternoon pretty little Mrs. Osborn looked into our state room door and asked us if we would not be kind enough to read to her while she sewed. We at once gave her a seat, and taking down a copy of the *Lady of the Lake*, read the first canto.

It was a real pleasure to read to her, she showed so much interest in the poem, and made such sensible and intelligent remarks upon it. We hope that she will call again.

Sat., Jan. 27th. Last evening immediately after supper the party went on the hurricane deck. It was really the first pleasant evening that we have enjoyed since leaving New York. The sea was smooth, and the *Continental* rocked gently, in it like a cradle. Fresh sea breezes made the air cool and pleasant, while old Mother Moon looked smilingly down casting her soft quiet rays on the little party. Some of the more quiet ones gathered together in little groups and passed away the time in pleasant gossip. One of the lively girls came up to us soon after going on deck and asked if we could not help to get up some excitement? "How would you like Copenhagen?" "Oh, that will be splendid," she replied, "perfectly splendid!" And soon a little party were gathered, and the game commenced. Some of the officers joined the party. The game was at its height when Mr. Mercer made his appearance, and commanded the party to desist playing. Some of the girls asked him what harm there was in their enjoying a little innocent amusement? He replied that he had no objection to the game itself, but it was against his strict orders for them not to associate with the officers. The play for the time being was broken up, and the party breaking up into couples commenced a promenade. Several of the girls, casting a look of defiance at Mercer, accepted the proffered arms of the officers, and took particular pains to walk by him as often as they could during the promenade. After a while some of the party went below and commenced a game of whist. Mr. Mercer, who seems to be always on the alert to discover the short comings of his party, followed them down, and waiting until the game was fairly commenced, burst upon the party and demanded why it was that they dared to infringe upon his orders against card playing? One of the gentlemen rose and demanded of Mercer an apology for the insult. "I did not wish to insult you Sir," said Mercer, "but these ladies know that I am opposed to card playing on principle, and I have strictly forbidden them to [be] engaged in any game." "Oh, let's give up the game and not have any fuss," exclaimed one of the girls. The gentleman compelled Mr. Mercer to apologize for his language and then put the cards in his pocket. Having accomplished, as he thought, his object Mr. Mercer went on deck in search of one of the girls to whom he was becoming very much devoted. He soon found her, and in a few minutes became entirely oblivious to all else on ship board. One of the card party who had followed him on deck, soon returned to the party, and reporting progress, the game was recommenced and finished. At ten o'clock Mr. Mercer awoke from his dream of bliss, and hunting up the Captain asked him if he did not think that it would be a good plan for the ladies to go to bed at 10 o'clock? "I think that it would be a very good plan Sir," said the Captain, "but Mr. Mercer if you can get them into bed at that time you can do more than I can." Mr. Mercer tried it on. Going on deck he laid his hand on the shoulder of one of the girls, and exclaimed "Go down and go to bed." "I won't," answered the fair one, and breaking away from him rushed to the other end of the boat. The excitement soon became general. The girls commenced promenading up and down the deck, exclaiming, as they passed Mercer, "Go to bed! Go to bed!" And go to bed they didn't till they got ready. To-day the books appropriated by the Book Sellers of New York for the particular use and benefit of the Virgins during the long voyage were placed upon the shelves today.[27] Among the works contributed were some very fine Editions of Standard authors. Mercer took particular pains that these volumes should remain boxed, and when asked for his reasons, replied that they [were] too valuable for the Virgins to handle, and he didn't mean to have them injured. When the more common class of books were ready to be given out, one of the girls came up and after looking at them for a few minutes, exlaimed "Mercer has got lots of books ain't he?" "Yes!" exclaimed another, "and Mr. Mercer has a mammoth brain."

Sunday, Jan. 28th. This morning Mercer went through the farce of holding a religious service. Most of the Virgins sat in the back part of the saloon and either devoted themselves to reading or amused themselves with making up faces at Mercer. When the services were about half through, one of the Engineers appeared at the door of the saloon and beckoned to one of the Virgins to come out. She started at once and rushing past Mr. Mercer, completely destroyed the serenity of that gentleman's temper by overthrowing his stand and scattering the sheets of his sermon, which had not been bound together, in all directions. He cast one angry glance in direction of the departing Virgin, and closed with a hasty prayer, and although he did not use the words, yet we knew that in his thoughts he was saying "Cass her eyes! Cass her eyes!"[28]

Jan. 29th. Last night between 6 and 7 o'clock, as the Virgins were eating their supper, while in Lat. 15-5 and Long. 44-36, the cry "A man over board,"[29] was heard from the fore part of the ship. All was excitement in a moment and every exertion was put forth to rescue the unfortunate man. He was a good swimmer and had the presence of mind to strike away from the ship, well knowing that if carried to the rear one blow from the shaft of the screw would be instant death. A life preserver was thrown to him, but it is feared that it failed to reach him, as at the time it was thrown he was struck by a heavy wave, which carried him a long distance from the ship's side. We were running at the time 10 knots an hour, and before the steamer could be stopped and the boats lowered he must have been at least a mile in the rear. The boat was out about two hours, but failed to find any trace of him. The steamer cruised for a long time over the spot, but not a sign of the missing man could be found. The sea was very rough at the time and he probably did not live 10 minutes after he struck the water.[30] The Virgins wept over his death, for there was one man less for them to flirt with. This morning "Pontoon" got decidedly belligerent. One of the little Warrens becoming angry at some thing she had said to him, told her to go to a very bad place. She at once became very angry in turn and told him if he gave her any more "fuss" she would tear his eyes out and give him a h_____ of a black eye &c. Mrs. W. was passing at the time and overheard the remark, and some very high words passed between them. Mrs. W. called Pontoon a low lived scrub. At which Pontoon flew into a violent passion, and told the former, that she could not only lick her son, but could also comb out her, Mrs. W.'s, hair with a three legged stool if she wished. At this interesting point two of the ladies interfered and the parties were separated.

Notes

1. The text of Mercer's circular, which bore the date of September 8, 1865 and which was issued by the office of the New England Aid Company of Boston, was included in a news item in the *New York Times*. Signed by Edward Everett Hale, chairman of the Pacific Committee, and by A. S. Mercer, emigrant agent for Washington Territory, this little sheet stated that "we do not advertise this emigration in the newspapers, because we only wish a class of emigrants who will improve the religious morals and tone of society in the T. None but those who can furnish us with references need apply" (*New York Times*, January 26, 1866, p. 2). Later, when many of the women changed their minds about going, Mercer did send letters to both the *Tribune* and the *Times* announcing that there was still room for passengers and stating the fare, and so forth (*New York Daily Tribune*, December 14, 1865, p. 6, and *New York Times*, December 16, 1865, p. 4). There was also the small brochure Mercer wrote to publicize the territory; A. S. Mercer, *Washington Territory, The Great North-West* (Utica, N.Y.: Childs, 1865), 38 pp.

2. "The number of persons on board was an even hundred, exclusive of officers and crew, the two new-born babes and four passengers for Rio de Janeiro. . . .The party consisted of five childless couples, six couples with two or three children, seven widows with offspring numbering from one to three, three unencumbered widows, one woman with two children, thirty-six unmarried women and fourteen single men" (Flora Pearson Engle, "The Story of the Mercer Expedition," *Washington Historical Quarterly*, VI [October, 1915], 232, hereafter referred to as Engle).

3. The *Times* version had this added: "We happened to be acquainted with some of them and being looked upon as a man of truth, our entrance into the parlor. . ." (*New York Times*, April 22, 1866, p. 5).

4. Add here from the *Times:* ". . .we could only think of coal and pork, both of which we assured them were safely stowed away in their proper places aboard ship. To our relief a message was received from Capt. Winsor, 'to get the ladies aboard at once' " (*ibid.*).

5. This was William F. Watkins, a California miner and legislator. A newspaper item described him: "Concerning Mr. Watkins. . .a correspondent sends us the following note. 'The man Watkins whose death was recently announced in your columns as having taken place in Panama [January 26, 1878], was an Assemblyman from Siskiyou county in the 1859 session of the California Legislature. Before his election to that body he had established quite a reputation as a correspondent of the *Sacramento Daily Union*, his letters being marked by terseness, reliability, and philosophic humor equal to that of Josh Billings. His nom de plume was "Sniktaw," (Watkins reversed). So famous had he become through his writings to the *Union* that the anxiety to see him on his arrival at the Capitol was as great as that at the advent of Senator Bones' " (*Sacramento Daily Union*, February 19, 1878, p. 3).

6. This was the number of women Mercer originally had hoped to take west with him.

7. Sniktaw brought suit in a San Francisco court and was successful in recovering goods purchased with his money. This left Mercer without the means of paying his San Francisco bills (*Sacramento Daily Union*, May 4, 1866, p. 3).

8. The *Times* item had this added: "And Mr. Mercer, Capts. Dall, Bermingham and Winsor went into the Captain's office to arrange the matter. When everything was in readiness, Capt. Bermingham sent all the passengers below and. . .called them up one by one and selected those who were to be sent ashore" (*New York Times*, April 22, 1866, p. 5).

9. Conant to the *Times:* "We learn that part of these persons had received a half promise that they might go provided the necessary arrangements could be made for their accommodation. Others had been absolutely refused passage, but came on board determined to defy the powers that be, and go scot free. They were all notified before the ship sailed that they could not go, and got their pains for the trouble—Some were unfortunately left behind, but as they were all notified, it was their own fault if they failed to reach the ship in time. We fear that some persons will make use of this unfortunate affair in trying to injure the character of Mr. Mercer and the enterprise in which he is engaged. He will soon vindicate himself before the public" (*ibid.*).

10. The *Times* version differed: "No resistance was made, although there was some pretty hard talking" (*ibid.*).

11. This man was probably William Carleton. A man by that name filed a deposition in a New York city court stating that he had come, through the inducement of Mercer, from Maine with his wife and children, and that although he had paid the passage money agreed upon for himself and family, they had all been left behind, destitute in New York (*ibid.,* January 31, 1866, p. 8).

12. This episode was not reported in the *Times* or in *Social Voices.* Flora Pearson Engle mentioned it and said that "Mr. Mercer was lying low in the coal bin and was not to be found" (Engle, p. 229).

13. Delicacy may have deterred Conant from recording one mishap, or perhaps he was just too busy helping someone to the rail to notice, but Ida May Barlow Pinkham recalled many years later: "Each day of the trip passed uneventfully by, the only serious calamity happened on the second day out when one of the girls lost her false teeth overboard in a moment of anguish rather common to travelers on the ocean, and for three months until we reached San Francisco, she was called toothless" (Ida May Barlow Pinkham, Family Records and Reminiscences of Washington Pioneers [Compiled by the Daughters of the American Revolution, typescript in Eastern Washington Historical Society], II, 220, hereafter cited as Ida May Barlow Pinkham).

14. The *Times* version: ". . .and his quiet cheerful manner soon had the effect of quieting their feelings and inducing them to return to their staterooms and try to sleep" (*New York Times,* April 22, 1866, p. 5).

15. Also from the *Times:* ". . .up the hatchway where, most fortunately for her, she was met on the last stair by the man of the *Times,* who succeeded in convincing her that the ship was all right" (*ibid.*).

16. The *Times* version also read "widder." This is a little word play with a line from Cowper's *The Timepiece* which reads "Oh, for a lodge in some vast wilderness" (*Oxford Dictionary of Quotations* [London, New York, and Toronto: Oxford University Press, 1953], p. 162).

17. In another description of the type of passenger, we read: "As we recovered our normal condition we began to look about us. With great satisfaction we found that we had a party of intelligent, amiable, sprightly people. The unmarried ladies are mostly from New England, and can boast a fair share of beauty, grace and culture, which characterize the best society of that region. It is impossible that the lovely girls who are with us should have left the East because their chances of matrimony were hopeless. One must look for some other reason" (Harriet Stevens, *Puget Sound Daily,* [Seattle], May 30, 1866, p. 2).

18. "Others called her 'spepsy' " (Engle, p. 236).
19. "There was also the dignified damsel who made the remark at the opening of the journey that she would 'clothe herself in her reserve, throw herself back upon her dignity, and remain so.' Events afterward transpired that caused some to wonder as to whether her whilom prop had not suddenly given way" (*ibid.*, p. 233).
20. The younger brother died before the *Continental* reached San Francisco. "Died: Conant. On Wednesday morning, April 11, John C. Conant, in the 13th year of his age. Funeral on Friday afternoon at 4½ o'clock, at the residence of his father, Dr. T. J. Conant, No. 163 Washington St., Brooklyn" (*New York Times*, April 13, 1866, p. 3).
21. This was Henry Ward Beecher of Plymouth Church, Brooklyn, New York. "Mr. Beecher kept a reporter in his church and then later edited and published his sermons. Sharp, racy, humorous utterances, keen remarks, sentences thrown off in the heat of speaking, witticisms that shook the Plymouth audiences as the forest leaves are shaken by the wind, were often missed in the public report" (N. A. Shenstone, *Anecdotes of Henry Ward Beecher* [Chicago: R. R. Donelley and Sons, 1887] pp. 173-74).
22. According to the *Times* report, the school teacher was "Little Miss [Harriet] Stevens" (*New York Times*, April 22, 1866, p. 5).
23. The one passenger with the title of Dr. before his name was Charles Barnard.
24. She left the ship at Rio.
25. Harriet Stevens was not disturbed by the food: "Our food is not luxurient but quite varied and abundant" (*Washington Standard* [Olympia], June 16, 1866, p. 1). However, Flora Pearson Engle, then a girl of fifteen, complained bitterly about the provisions at the time, but many years later said: "It was surely a seemingly great hardship at the time, but the writer has often wondered if our rigid diet was not a blessing in disguise; certain it was that in our voyage of over three months duration not one of the hundred passengers was sick" (Engle, p. 230).
26. Another version: " 'Oh! we are a little selfish in this matter,' she laughingly replied, 'It is not so much for Mr. Mercer as it is to make an impression on the young men of the country to which we are going, and make them think we are splendid housekeepers' " (*Social Voices*, February 18, 1869). The *Times* report had in addition: "These shirts and stockings are to be offered for sale at a great fair which at some future day is to come off at Seattle" (*New York Times*, April 22, 1866, p. 5). The Peebles girls were not cooperative in this matter. Because they had paid their full passage they felt they were like passengers on any other ship, and therefore, not required to do Mercer's bidding. "My sister and I did not get on very well with him. He wanted to arrange plans for us.... He had brought along a stock of yarns, cloth and other materials, which he distributed to the girls...but my sister and I did not care to have things given us to make" (Anna Peebles Brown, MS interview, Sophie Frye Bass Library, Seattle Historical Society).
27. "Peter Cooper met Mercer and donated a library for the *Continental*" (*San Francisco Examiner*, June 25, 1893, p. 15).
28. Cass—to render useless (now obsolete). R. C. Trench as quoted in *Modern Eclectic Dictionary of the English Language* (New York: Collier's, 1905), I, 870.
29. This sad occurrence was noticed by the newspapers: "One sailor was lost 375 miles north of the Equator on the Atlantic side" (*Puget Sound Weekly* [Seattle], May 21, 1866, p. 5).

30. More regarding this: "Fortunately no deaths occurred save the drowning of one of the deck hands, and that incident was sad in the extreme. The man in some way had incurred the displeasure of the first mate, who paid his grudge by cutting almost in twain one of the ropes in the ladder in the rigging and then sending the sailor aloft for some purpose. The rope broke and the unfortunate man fell in the water. . . .The mate was afterwards placed in confinement. . ." (Engle, p. 230).

2

PETTICOAT FEVER

XXXXXXXXXXXXXXXXXXXXXXXXXXXXXXXXXXXXXXXXXXXXXXXXXXXXXXXX

THIS AFTERNOON a sighing swain came to grief, and it was no less a personage than Mr. Mercer himself. Long before the steamer sailed and since the party came on board it has been his boast that he was an incorrigible old bachelor, and that there was no fair lady among the entire party who could draw from his heart those exquisite lines of Shakespeare,

> "Is't possible that on so little acquaintance
> You should like her? That but seeing
> You should love her? & loving woo?"[1]

He is the only young man in the party who has bowed the knee to Cupid's shrine. There is on board a young maiden of good report and fair to look upon. She is on her way to Washington Territory to teach, who or what, no one seems to know, as there are nothing but men in that country and Mr. Mercer probably entertaining the same view, thought that he could not do better than to offer her the shelter of his own wings, and teach her the pleasures which are centered in a log cabin among the pine forests of Washington Territory. Poor deluded young man! He imagined that simply because he was the agent of this expedition, that all the virgins were desperately in love with him, and were only waiting for him to offer himself, to fly into his arms. Without giving this young virgin the slightest intimation of what he was about to do, not even so much as a tender look, or an evening's courtship, he invited her into his state room this morning, and telling her that he loved her enough to marry her, opened his arms and smiled fondly upon her. The maiden laughed right in his face, and opening the door rushed from the state [room], leaving the disconsolate swain, the perfect picture of astonishment and discomfiture. "Where now so fast," we asked as she rushed past. "Oh! don't stop me," she exclaimed, "the old fool wants to marry me, and I hate the very sight of him." Mr. Mercer being a firm believer in the old proverb "Faint heart ne'er won fair lady," vigorously followed up his suit. He sent her a note this afternoon, full of pretty little speeches made only by young men who are laboring under that disease so prevalent among young men, and known as "Petticoats on the brain," and in closing stated that he did not think that she understood her own mind. That if she would only consent to embark with him on the shingle of matrimony, they would sail together, as happy as two cooing doves, down life's dark surging waves. If she still refused he would consider it a great favor if she would return the note. As soon as she had read it she walked up to the sighing swain, who at [the] moment was talking to some ladies, and handing him the note, said, "Here is your note old Pap." It was too much even for Mercer. Completely overwhelmed and disgusted with the world and young school marms in particular, he took to his bed, and at the present time the petticoat fever has complete possession of his brain.

Tuesday, Jan. 30th. Some of the young officers as well as the young men have fallen into the bad habit lately, of spending the bright moon light evenings, on deck, with their arms round the waist of some fair virgin. There is no particular harm in it if done from right motives, but there are some high spirited girls whose feelings of delicacy revolt at any such attempts at familiarity. There are some such girls on board of this ship and they have drawn the line and woe to the young man who attempts to step over it. While one of these girls was sitting on the hurricane deck this afternoon sewing, the 2d Engineer came and sat down by her side. After a few minutes conversation he passed his arm quietly round her waist. Quick as a flash she buried her needle half its length in his arm. He gave a loud "ouch" of disgust and exclaimed, "What made you do that?" "Your arm was not in its right place, Sir," she quietly replied as she gathered up her work and went below. As she went down a maidenly looking lady came on deck and seated her self near us. She has a very pleasant looking face, and looks as if she would have made a real nice Mother to a large family of children. "Do you know Mr. Conant," she said turning towards us, "what I am going to do when I get to Washington Territory?" "I suppose that you will marry some nice old bachelor and devote the balance of your existence to making his miserable life happy," we replied. "Indeed, I shall not," she replied. "I am going to be the Missionary of the Territory." "Yes, but do you know that the old bachelors of W.T. are said to be a very fascinating set of mortals, and that it is utterly impossible to resist their charms. I am afraid that you are entering upon a dangerous experiment. I wish you much joy in your work, only bear in mind that Washington Territory is a very different place from Greenland's icy mountains and India's Coral Strand, and in your enthusiasm you may find yourself confining your labors to the conversion of one man, in which case be very careful that his squaw does not come up behind and take your scalp." The good lady seemed to be very much impressed with our remarks, and said if my representations were true she did not think that she would go any farther than San Francisco. "That is a bully pen you've got there Conant," [and] looking up we find "Pontoon" leaning over our shoulder. "Yes, Pontoon," we replied, "it is a spendid pen, and I prize it so much that I never lend it." "Be a good fellow and lend it to me to write a letter to my beau, and I will like you ever so much." "Will you return it as soon as you write the letter?" we asked. "Yes," she said, "in less than an hour." We handed her the pen with some misgivings as to the prospect of ever seeing it again. For some days past Sniktaw has been paying very close attention to the widow W. So close in fact that it came under the observation of Pontoon. Meeting the two walking together on the Port side this morning, she made a very low bow, and exclaimed, "Good morning Sniktaw, glad to see you playing the sweet to the Widder W." Sniktaw looked a little confused and Mrs. W. bit her lips in anger. About an hour after Sniktaw hunted up Pontoon and asked for an explanation. "Are you not going to marry her?" asked she. "Marry hell and brimstone," he replied. "I thought you was not so sick a fool," said she, turning from him to hunt up Mrs. W. Going to the latter's state room she peeped in and shouted out as loud as she could. "I asked Sniktaw if he was going to marry you and he said that he would sooner marry Hell and brimstone." It is not known how Sniktaw and the widow settled the matter between them, but it is presumed that he denied the whole thing in toto.

Friday, Feb. 2d. As we expected Mr. Mercer's sickness was not unto death, although he has been very sick, "of school marms." When the fever was said to be at its height, a very old maid went into the state room to take a look at the sick man. He was lying remarkably quiet for one who had trouble on the brain. She took his hand; a bright smile parted his lips and in a tender loving voice he breathed the name of the young lady who had called him "Old Pap." Oh! Wasn't he furious when he opened his eyes and found out to whom it was he was using such loving language, and in an angry voice told her that she ought to be in better business than coming into a gentleman's room when he was asleep. The lady in dismay beat a hasty retreat, and soon in the midst of a circle of sympathizing friends, gave her opinion of Mr. Mercer. Mrs. P____ who is always full of fun and frolic said that she would soon make the man a great deal sicker than he really was. So she ran into his state room and exclaimed in a doleful voice; "I am real sorry that you are love sick and are you not sorry to[o] Mr. Mercer that you are so love sick? Isn't it a pity that a poor old man like you cannot find some girl to love him." The endless amount of gossip which his love affair gave rise to and the immense amount of ridicule to which it subjected him, brought about a sudden cure, and today he called them all together and made a very foolish speech. Taking his text from the 3d Chapter of James and 2d verse (he always took a text when he wanted to make a speech) he dilated long if not eloquently on their minding their own business and not meddle with his. It is an old saying that a sore heart doeth many foolish things and it was abundantly proved in this case for instead of putting a bridle on their tongues it only made the Virgins talk the more.

This afternoon pretty little Mrs. O____ made her appearance at our door, and asked us if we would not be kind enough to finish the "Lady of the Lake." "Most certainly," we replied. Giving her our steamer chair, we took a stool and sitting down by her side commenced. The sea was in one of her ugly moods, and every few minutes the steamer would give one of those sudden lurches, which would have thrown the little lady out of the chair upon the deck, if we hadn't prevented it by catching her round the waist, and bracing our feet firmly against the sides of the state room. The whole scene was of a most interesting character. While we were reading Sniktaw and Mrs. W. joined the group, and soon after Pontoon made her appearance. She was always round when she was least wanted. She looked at us for a moment and then said, "Well! If you four ain't the sickest lookin couple I ever did see. You look decidedly healthy." Mrs. W. made an angry retort, but Mrs. ____ laughed and told Pontoon that she was jealous. In a former place we said something about Mercer's calling one of the virgins into his state room and lecturing her on the sin of flirting with the officers and the probable consequence arising there from. She gave us a little account of her conversation with the old man (the virgins call him, although he says that he is not yet 30).[2] A portion of the conversation is not fit to be written and any man who will pour it into the ears of a young girl deserves to be thrown over board. In substance he told her that every officer on board had designs on them, and if the girls gave them any chance would certainly prove their ruin. The young lady who is pretty high spirited, told him that she had seen something of the world and was abundantly able not only to select her own company but to take care of herself. That she did not consider him a bit better than the officers, and that he was simply jealous because he was not as good looking as they were and consequently was not as attractive to the girls.

Mr. Mercer asked her if she did not consent to place herself under his charge and be guided by his advice? She said that she was willing to place herself under his charge and take his advice so long as he conducted himself as a gentleman, but not otherwise unless he would consent to refund the money which she had paid him for her passage. Mercer couldn't see that part of the programme, and she left him with the declaration that she should flirt with the officers as much and as long as she pleased and that she should like to see him prevent her. He tried it on but soon got very sick of it, and today he told us that he looked upon Miss _____ as a ruined girl. We told him that we entertained a different opinion; that girls of her spirit generally managed to look out for no. one. The purser of the steamer owns a dog, a great over grown mongrel cur, ungainly and awkward in all her movements. She looks more like an elephant than a dog. All the ladies except Pontoon have taken a strong dislike to her. Pontoon probably fancies the dog on account of the owner. Today one of the ladies give the cur a kick and exclaimed, "Get out, you homely man's dog." Pontoon was standing by at the time and throwing her arms round the animal's neck, exclaimed, "she is a pretty man's dog. She is a pretty man's dog! and you shall not hurt her."

"Are you busy Mr. C?" "No, not very, Miss G_____. What can I do for you?" "I want you to write some verses in my autograph album." "Oh! I cannot do that. I never wrote a poem in my life, but I can give you my autograph if you want." Miss G_____ looked a little disappointed and said that an autograph without verses wouldn't be a bit nice, and that she thought I might do it. To please her I took the book, with a sigh, and many misgivings as to the result. I went to my room and after an hour or two hard work succeeded in grinding out the following lines.

Once while looking in the west,
Watching the sunset's glowing ray;
A lady touched me on the vest,
And thus in accents soft did say!
Here is a book in which I keep,
The autographs of all my friends.
I want some verses from your pen,
Which are sweeter when they come from men.
We took the book, and with a sigh,
In agony did thus reply:
I'm not a poet born to song,
But simply a prosy thing of earth.
To attempt to sing would be a wrong,
For in music there's no second birth.
So I'll not try to rhyme,
But simply write my name,
So that in all future time,
I can your closest friendship claim.

Signing our name, we took the book to her and said that it was the best that we could do. She seemed perfectly satisfied, which was a great comfort.

Feb. 3d. Last night Mr. R. called to us to come on deck and see the southern cross. It was one of the most beautiful sights that we ever saw. You cannot see this collection of stars this side of the Equator. We will not stop to describe it now. A full description of it can be found in Her[s]chel. We crossed the Equator today, and many of the girls were thrown into the greatest trepidation by the mate's telling them that before they went to bed they would probably receive a visit from Old Father Neptune. Pontoon was particularly threatened but she laughed and said that she was ready for him. We told old High Daddy that a special arrangement had been made with Father Neptune to give him a special hearing. The old fellow was fearfully worked up and at once went off and told his wife, who came to us at once and said that if her man had any tricks played on him, she would beat our head with a flat iron. This morning one of the girls caught up old High Daddy's baby, and exclaimed, "Oh, my little Darling I wish that you was mine!" "I know of only one way to get them," replied the old sinner, looking at her with a wicked lear in his eye. The girl dropped the poor little wretch on the deck, and rushed below.

We walked into the Purser's office this afternoon and the first thing that struck our eye was our gold pen. "Halloo! D____," we exclaimed, "How did our gold pen come here?" "Your gold pen!" said D____, "the deuce that's your gold pen." "I will describe and prove that it is mine," we answered a little angrily, "and what is more I lent it to Pontoon the other day to write a letter with, and that is the last that I have seen of it till now." "Is that so," said D____ laughing. "Why she brought me the pen this morning and made me a present of it saying that she had no use for it. However, if it is yours take it." A few minutes after we met Pontoon and told her that we had found our pen in the purser's room. She looked rather confused for a moment, and then bursting into a loud laugh, told us that she was happy to hear it.

Feb. 4th. The only one who suffered any from the visit of old Father Neptune was the old Doctor. The poor old gentleman had got hold of a bottle of fine brandy in the afternoon, and about eight o'clock in the evening was two thirds in the wind. Some of the boys in the fore castle under the leadership of the Junior Officers laid a plan for giving him a regular washing down. One of the Quartermasters, a regular wag, laid himself in the bunk, and sent for the Dr in great haste as he was in great pain. The old Doctor's good wife hustled him out of bed as soon as she heard that one of the men was sick, and as soon as he was able to comprehend the situation, one of the boys led him down into the fore castle. The Dr gave the sick man a careful examination and then decided that he must be opened and his bowels taken out. At this announcement the man could keep his face no longer and laughing aloud jumped out of the bunk and ran away, followed by his comrades, after first blowing out the light. Some one gave a whistle as a signal that everything was in readiness and two or three from above poured half a dozen pails of salt water on the head of their victim. For half a minute everything was quiet, and some feared that the boys had finished the Dr but he soon sang out "Keep his bowels open, boys, the port holes are out and we'll all go to sea."

He soon made his appearance and the way he pitched into every body, would soon have given him many patients, but the Captain happened along at that time and led him away. He stopped at the door of the upper saloon, and one of the officers went to him and complained of a severe pain in the head. The Dr cast a look of contempt upon him and said "Have you not got a pain in your toe? If you have I can lick you or ten thousand more men like you." Last night the first baby was born on board the *Continental.* The happy father,[3] a young shoemaker brought her up in his arms this morning for us to look at, and asked if we did not think that it was the finest looking girl that we had ever seen? For fear of receiving a terrible thrashing if we made a different answer, we told him that she was a regular rouser. The answer seemed to satisfy him.

Here comes another virgin with a book in her hand. I fear that it is another autograph album and says I to myself, Roger Conant, you have got yourself into business now. "Oh! Mr. C. Those verses that you wrote for Miss G____'s album were beautiful and I shall insist upon your writing some in mine. Write anything you please only make it rhyme." Knowing that there was no help for it we took the book and wrote as follows:

> When you leave this earthly nest,
> When stifled is your latest groan
> May you upon Old Abram's breast
> Appear before the Saviour's throne.

She was perfectly satisfied. And we are very much satisfied to hear that there [are] no more Autograph Albums on board.

Feb. 10th. We are at last off Rio de Janeiro.[4] Last night while standing on deck we saw what we thought to be a new star just above the horizon, and turning to Mr. R. who stood by, asked him the name of it. He laughed and said that it was the Light House at Cape Frio, and that it was about 40 miles distant. We watched the light as it grew larger and larger. We passed the cape about 4 in the morning, and a wicked looking place it was. A great many vessels were wrecked here before this light house was built. The approach to the harbor of Rio is perfectly beautiful. On the right rises Serra Dos Orgos range. There is nothing wild or grand in the scenery of these mountains as seen from the ocean, but they have a real dreamy home like look, and the sea worn traveler whose eyes for many long and weary days have looked out upon an unbroken waste of waters, as he gazes upon them experiences a feeling of relief and repose, and he feels indeed that he is approaching a haven of rest. On the left are several rocky isles rising abruptly out of the sea. How come they there out in the wide ocean with no companion to bear them company? Perhaps they are the bones of the old man of the mountains, and were sent by him to act as sentinels over the entrance to the harbor. But who is this old man of the mountains? Turn your eye to the left and you will see him stretched out upon his mountain bed, in majestic repose, his strongly masked features sharply delineated against the sky. Never before have we seen so singular a phenomena in nature, and it seemed as if a sculptors skilful hands had been at work chisling out those features.[5] Right at his feet and at the entrance of the harbor looms up the steep sides of the Sugar Loaf Mountain. He looks like a sharp old fellow, and no doubt keeps vigilant watch over the entrance to see that no unwelcomed intruder gains admittance. Nature has been very liberal in her gifts to Rio, and upon these hills and mountains fortifications could be erected, such as would defy all the powers of the earth, except the United States. Yet all the defense that Rio can boast of for the present is a miserable fort, which a Yankee gun boat could batter down in a hour. We soon reached our anchorage inside the harbor about half a mile from the town. What a beautiful picture is here spread out before us. Turn your eyes in what ever direction you will, you discover something beautiful to admire. Mountains and high ranges of hills encircle the harbor giving it the appearance of a mountain lake. It extends some thirty miles inland and is completely studded with beautiful islands. The shore is one glittering beach; sometimes standing out in bold relief then and retreating into the green recesses of deep ravines over hung by stupendous cliffs which cast their dark shadows on the waters below. No idea of the town can be had from the harbor and it has more the appearance of a small straggling village, than a large city of 400,000 inhabitants. South of the city are situated the residences of some of the more wealthy citizens. Many of these residences are built after the style of the old Spanish castles, and being located among these hills they make a picturesque and romantic appearance. Shortly after coming to anchor an order was issued that no one must leave the ship until after the return of Capt. Winser and Mr. Mercer. Mr. M. did not return until late in the evening so that nothing was said about going on shore that night. The next morning dawned bright and beautiful and at 9 o'clock the great Head of the family called his little flock together to expound to them that most useful of all maxims "Children obey your parents." He told them how deeply interested he felt in their welfare, so much so that he could not bear them out of his sight for a single moment. He said that he had consulted some of the leading American merchants in the city, and learned that it was in a very unhealthy condition; that cholera and small pox were raging to a fearful extent, making it very unsafe for the ladies to go on shore. Fear came into his eyes when he told them how willing he was to traverse the streets of the city alone facing disease and even death itself in order to find out where it would be safe for them to go. He closed by saying that although he did [not] wish to place any severe restrictions upon them they must distinctly understand that they could not go on shore in company with any gentleman except himself. He thought that he had the girls in a tight place, and we shall see how well he succeeded. Murmurs low but deep were heard on every side, although at first there were

no open expressions of insubordination at the time.[6] In about two hours
two of the girls appeared in company with two of the officers and attempted
to get into the boat, but they were stopped by the 2d Mate who told them
that he had strict orders to allow no ladies to go on shore without permission from the Captain. The officers at once went to the latter & asked to
be allowed to take the girls to the city. The Captain laughed and told them
that they must ask Mr. Mercer. The officers made up their minds that
it was a gone case, but resolved to make the trial and try and carry the
forlorn hope. "Oh! certainly," said Mr. Mercer, "you can take them on shore
only promise me to bring them back safe before sundown." The officers
promised, and off went the party in high glee, amid the waving of handkerchiefs from the ladies and cheers from the boys. Taking down his bars
to let out two of his lambs the rest we are afraid will press him so hard
that he will find it impossible to put them up again. In the afternoon as
the sun began to sink behind the western hills, Mr. Mercer went on the
hurricane deck and commenced straining his eyes towards the city to catch
a glimpse of the returning party. "What are you looking at Mr. Mercer?"
asked the Captain in a rather sarcastic tone. "I am looking for that party,"
said Mr. Mercer. "They said that they would be back before sundown."
"If you see them by twelve o'clock tonight you will do well," laughed the
Captain, "for my part I shouldn't be surprised if they did not come back
tonight." "I will never let the officers take them to the city again," muttered
Mercer. "You have made the same remark before," said the Captain as he
walked away. At one o'clock the sound of the oars was heard and the party
soon appeared on deck. "Where is old Red Head?" asked Pontoon who was
one of the party. "After breathing out theatenings and slaughter for two
or three hours he has gone to his rest," we replied. "Have you had a nice
time?" "Bully," said she, "Bully," and down she went to her state room followed by the other girl.

Monday, Feb. 12th. We arrived just too late to witness the Carnival.
It was a great disappointment to all the party. Early this morning we went
on shore with Captain Winser, and made our way up to the Commission
house of Thomas B. Baldwin & Co. Their house is the favorite resort of
Americans coming to this port and we had the pleasure of meeting with
a large number of officers from the U.S. Steamers *Shamokin* and *Onward*
and also Captains of merchant vessels all manifested an anxious interest
in the character of the cargo on board of the *Continental* as they were pleased
to call the girls. We gave them all the information in our power, and invited [them] to visit the steamer and examine for them selves. They all

accepted, and we haven't the slightest doubt but that they will keep it. Both Captain Baldwin and Captain Walker gave us a very cordial invitation to make their store our headquarter[s] while the steamer remained in port. In our rambles about the city Captain Baldwin acted as our pilot and we are indebted to him for a great deal [of] valuable information.

Rio de Janeiro – is built after the style of old Spanish towns and is as antiquated and old fashioned as the most dilapidated old fogy could desire. The streets are narrow, crooked and dirty and are built without the slightest regard to taste or comfort. They perfectly swarm with negroes, and you can hardly turn with running against them. Most of those that you meet in the streets are of the very lowest order and they present a most forlorn and disgusting appearance. The men generally wear nothing but a light pair of pantaloons fastened round the waist with a leather strap. From the waist up everything is bare not even a cap to cover their wooly pates. Most of these negroes are slaves, and their present low condition is, in a great measure, their own fault. The slave code of Brazil is very liberal, and gives the slave, who has any ambition to improve his condition both socially and politically, every advantage. Any slave who desires freedom can, after a certain number of years, purchase it if he has money, and they have many ways of earning it.[7] If he and his master cannot agree upon a price, the Government appoint a commissioner who decides the question and his decision is final. No matter where he came from or how menial his condition as a slave, he can by industry and frugality rise to high positions in the Government. If he succeeds in accumulating wealth he can marry into the most influential families in the country. The chief mode of public conveyance is by small hacks drawn by one mule. The streets are so narrow that these hacks occupy nearly the entire width of the street, leaving just passage enough for foot passengers, who can escape being run over by standing up very straight against the sides of the houses. They have no carts in Rio, to carry goods. All labor of this kind is performed by negroes and it is wonderful to see the amount which one of them will carry on his head. You may look here in vain for a milk cart, not one of those necessary appendages to society can be seen anywhere. But here comes a cow; perhaps she can enlighten us upon the subject. The man who drives her utters a peculiar cry, and out rushes a man from a house with a small tin cup in his hand. The driver sits down and milks the cup full, receives his little piece of silver, and then starts his cow in search of another customer. The Exchange was the only place of interest that we visited today. It is a large room plainly furnished with long tables and common wooden chairs. At these tables were seated men of all nations earnestly engaged in discussing the state of the money market. The Brokers' offices are little stalls, each containing a desk. These stalls were divided off from the main room by a high iron railing. Every merchant doing business in the city is required to be a member of the Board and is expected to be on change at least once during the day.

Tuesday, Feb. 13th. "Are you asleep my dear?" "Kiss me my love," were sweet words which fell upon the ears of the cook last night as he lay in his berth. He was a great fool, for instead of throwing his arms round the speaker, and holding her till he could find out who she was, he simply growled out "who are you?" The fair one, who ever she was, discovered that she had made a mistake and beat a hasty retreat into the darkness. This morning the cook told the story and everybody laughed at him for being such a fool. "Are you asleep my dear? Kiss me my love" is in the mouth of every lady and they all wonder who she can be, and probably the guilty one herself wonders more than all the rest, when the others are round. Yesterday Geo. Debro bought a monkey to hold water in to keep it sweet and fresh during the hot part of the day. These monkeys are made very much like a gourd, and will hold about half a gallon. It was very late when he came on board, and by mistake he got into old Auntie ____'s state room instead of his own. It was too dark to distinguish anything, and Geo. hung up his monkey, and taking off all his clothes except his drawers, and drawing aside the curtains of the berth placed his hands upon the placid features of old Mother ____, who softly pronounced the name of Sniktaw. Geo. waited to hear no more but seizing his clothes rushed [out] of her state room into his own. This morning Geo. was in great trouble because he could not find his monkey, and after giving every part of the steamer except Mrs. ____'s state room a thorough search, made up his mind that some of the girls had stolen it. "I think that it is very strange," said Miss Mary Bermingham, to us this morning, "that Geo. cannot find his monkey." "Where was Geo. last night?" we asked. "Do you believe," said she, "that he made a mistake and found himself in old Mrs. ____'s state room, and I do believe," she continued, "that the goose left it there." "Oh! Geo.," she exclaimed to that unhappy youth, who was walking about the deck in a most forlorn manner, "have you looked in Mrs. ____'s state room for your monkey?" Geo. did not wait to make reply, but soon returned bringing his monkey with him and just as happy as he could be. We went on shore at 9 o'clock in the Captain's boat, and the first place we visited was the market. It was kept much cleaner than our Eastern markets. The most beautiful sight to us was the large variety of tropical birds. We cannot begin to give their names, or the color of their plumage. We were so much interested in studying these birds that we did not pay much attention to anything else. As we were passing out of the market there rose up before us one of the most queenly figures that our eyes ever beheld. She was a fully developed negress. She had a truly royal carriage, and wore an elaborate white turban of immense size on her head. Her magnificent arms were bare to the shoulder and were covered with bracelets. A white, close fitting jacket and colored skirt completed her custom and she moved about as if perfectly conscious of her beauty. From the market we went to the custom house which is a place of much interest and well worth a visit. In the selection of officers and clerks no attention is paid to color, and the black man if he has money and influence can obtain as high a position as his white brother. During our visit a young fine looking and keen eyed mulatto entered the room. As soon as his presence became known all the clerks rose and saluting him remained standing until the salute was returned,—a custom utterly unknown in Democratic America.

He occupied a high position in the Custom House and was connected by marriage with one of the most influential families in the Empire. From the Custom House we went over to the Palace. It is a low heavy looking building with balustraded windows and stuccoed walls, and is utterly devoid of architectural beauty. It has more the appearance of a Lowel factory boarding house than the residence of an Emperor. The palace together with the Chapel where the family worship occupy two sides of a square and are so arranged that the family can pass from one to the other without being subjected to the gaze of the public.

The public wash basin is a large fountain standing in the centre of a large square from which gentle showers are thrown into a large basin which completely encircles it. Here all the poor of the city can come and do their washing without being charged for water. The Square is completely covered with green grass and is as soft as a velvet carpet. When we entered the Square two or three hundred people were collected there. Some were engaged in washing, while others were lying idly on the grass watching their more industrious companions. Some of the most ludicrous sights will often occur. These people seem to take the greatest delight in playing tricks on each other, but as all parties seem to enjoy the sport no ill feeling is created. We happened to be a witness to one, and to us it was a curious and novel sight. A poor negress was busily engaged over the basin, when a smart looking darky, with a merry twinkle in his eye, came up behind and seizing her by the feet plunged her head foremost into the foaming suds. At this mishap there was a general shout in which the unfortunate victim, as soon as she recovered herself, heartily joined. On returning to the steamer we found some of the ladies anxiously waiting for us. Some officer from the *Onward* had given them an invitation to go on shore and see the elephant. They were anxious to accept but the officers being two thirds in the wind, they were afraid to trust them selves with them alone. There was no help for it so we went back to the city. We were very sorry to see that Pontoon made one of the party. The 1st place that the officers took the party to was a large wholesale liquor store. We [were] taken into a back room. Six different kinds of wine were placed upon the table, and the officers set them selves to work to get the ladies tight. Two of them simply touched the wine to their lips, but Pontoon drank a full glass of each kind. Fearing that the hot close room would set her to sleep, we told the officers that it was time to start out in search of something else, to which they agreed.

We had hardly left the store when it began to rain, and we all ran into a large wholesale sugar house. The sugar barrels were placed in a circle round the room leaving a large open space in the middle. The fresh air had revived Pontoon a little, and she seemed to feel very happy. Raising her dress a little she danced a gig round the room and attempted to sing a song. The officer who had her in charge, feeling very much ashamed called a hack, and the party drove up town and had dinner, at which a great deal of wine was drank by the officers and Pontoon. The officers then thought that it was time to go out and take a walk. One officer with one of the ladies started down one street with Miss G____ and the other with Pontoon started down another leaving Mrs. C____ and Roger Conant to take care of themselves. "Oh! Mr. Conant," said Mrs. C____ "I can trust Miss G. but don't let that other officer get away with Pontoon. She has drank too much wine, and there is no knowing what will happen." "If you can walk fast enough, we will try and keep them in sight," we replied. So off we started and for three hours we walked the streets of Rio. At last we made a flank movement and succeeded in cutting them off. "It is time to go on board young folks," said Mrs. C____ and taking Pontoon by the arm she marched her down towards the wharf. The young officer swore a terrible oath. We told him that he was a fool which he acknowledged to be true. On reaching the boat we found Officer P. and Miss G____ waiting for us. P. was feeling the effects of the wine, and first made us a speech of congratulation on our safe arrival. He then sang a song, in which he

The Occidental Hotel in Seattle where Mercer's belles stayed upon arrival
(Museum of History and Industry, Seattle)

S.S. *Continental (Steamship Historical Society of America)*

"Mercer's Belles," a cartoon from *Puck, the Pacific Pictorial,* 1866 *(The Bancroft Library)*

said that he wouldn't go home till morning. We at last succeeded in getting them all into the boat, and started for the steamer. The young officer who had Pontoon in charge threw his arms round her neck and asked her if he might kiss her for her Mother. Pontoon at first told him to go to h____ and then laid her head on his shoulder. "Miss H____" exclaimed Mrs. C____, "if you have no respect for your self do have some respect for the rest of the party, and behave yourself." "Am 'havin myself," said Pontoon, "tend'n to own business, 'tend to you'n." She then started up "We won't go home till morning" and another which she called "We'll get as tight as a brick." We told Mrs. C. not to say anything to her as it would only make her worse. At this moment Officer P. who had been examining some packages, threw up his arms and exclaimed, "Here is the wine, and here are the crackers, but where in the name of God is the cheese!" "Luff, Sir luff,"[8] shouted one of the men, "we are running into this bark." "Luff it is," replied the officer, "but Miss G____ is here." We succeeded in getting the girls on board, and we told the younger officer that it was the last time we should ever go on shore with such a crowd again, to which he replied that he rather thought it was. He tried to follow Pontoon downstairs but the 1st Officer told him that it would not do, and that the best thing he could do would be to go back to his own ship. The young officer went into his boat threatening to send a challenge to McDougall.

Wednesday, Feb. 14th. A party of ladies went on shore this morning. They marched in solemn procession up the principal street, and created great excitement among the natives. Mr. Mercer was the leader of this interesting party, and the first place he took them to was the small pox hospital. Some of the ladies did not know what the building was used for till afterwards, and were very indignant at Mr. Mercer. As the party were crossing one of the large squares, the Royal carriage containing the Emperor and his family passed. As soon as the ladies learned who they were they all took out their handkerchiefs and waved them after the Royal family, who were very much amazed at this great breach of etiquette. In Rio no respectable woman is seen in the streets during the day, except in a carriage and then no notice is taken of them. Pontoon was invited to join the party but declined on the ground that she did not wish to be seen in Mr. Mercer's company. The first place we visited today was the Museum, which contains some beautiful specimens of Brazilian birds. There are also some very choice minerals from the mines. But the variety is not large, and we are afraid that it will not increase much as the people seem to show the same lack of enterprise in the cultivation of the fine arts as they do in the architectural construction of their buildings. We became tired of walking about the streets and calling a hack rode out to the Botanical Gardens. These gardens are a most delightful retreat from the heat and dust of the city, and large parties of gentlemen resort here with their families every evening. Every large city ought to have such a garden, where the people can go and amid trees and flowers find that repose and quiet which every mind, harassed by the daily duties of a business life so much needs. The scenery here is as wild and romantic as the most enthusiastic lover of nature could desire. In front of the garden you have a splendid view of the ocean, while right back of it rises the lofty sides of the Corcovado. It occupies an area of about 50 acres and is intersected with winding walks, which are over hung with different varieties of tropical trees.[9] There are large numbers of plots scattered over the grounds filled with the most beautiful shrubs and flowers. Becoming tired, we seated ourself on a large comfortable seat in a beautiful little grove. A fresh sea breeze cooled the air, and taking off our hat, we stretched ourself out at full length on the seat, and watched the waves as in majestic volume they rolled towards the shore, only to dash themselves upon the rocks and recede with a low murmering sound, as if angry in being thus foiled in their efforts to take possession. The setting sun warned us that it was time to go. We were highly delighted with our visit to these beautiful gardens, & in consideration of the pleasure which we derived from it, will forgive the Rio people for the balance of their short comings. On our return to the steamer we found a regular tempest in the family tea pot. Lieut. Raeney and another gay and festive officer from the U.S. Steamer *Shamokin* had come on board to invite two of the ladies to go on shore and have a time. Poor Raeney unfortunately lighted upon Pontoon. Now Pontoon and the young lady invited by the other officer are deadly enemies, the young lady considering Pontoon beneath her in every way, and declared that she should not go on shore in company with Pontoon under any consideration. Pontoon was willing to overlook "their vow," as she called it, for the sake of having a high time on shore. But the other one was obdurate and would not yield an inch, neither would she excuse the officer who gave her the invitation and make an arrangement for another day. She was determined to go on shore, and was equally determined that Pontoon should not go. Poor Raeney, who could not speak the language, and was dependent on his comrade, was in a very unhappy frame of mind, and he paced the hurricane deck not knowing what to do, and there we found him when we came on board. To us he at once confided his troubles and asked our advice as to what he should do? "That can be easily managed," we replied. "We'll get Pontoon to excuse you, you can then invite Miss B____. In the meantime while the girls are getting ready, you can row back to your ship and bring back Lieut. McFarland who is just the boy for Pontoon." Taking Pontoon [to] one side we told her that Raeney was a regular spoony; that he belonged to the church, and would sooner die than drink a glass of wine. The best thing she could do if she wanted to have a good time would be to excuse him, and we would send for Lieut. McFarland to take her to the city, and McFarland could stand up under more wine than any other man in Rio. "Mc is the boy for me," she exclaimed, "and I will excuse this poor Devil." Everything being arranged we rejoined the group. "I'll excuse you, Mr. Raeney," she said, "from takin me to the city, but I want you to understand that I'm a goin to stand before you in my true colors, and ain't a goin to make myself out to be any better than I really be. I make overcoats for a liven, and ain't dependent upon a Mother to keep a factory boarding house to support me." Miss B____ accepted Raeney's invitation and with a look of supreme satisfaction on his face he started after McFarland. The young lady then started to get ready, and some of the girls formed a row on each side through which she was compelled to pass, and they all exclaimed as she went by "make way for the Queen. Allow her royal majesty to pass." We don't blame the poor child one bit and think that she was right. Some one had been posting her about the scenes of the night before, probably Miss G____. In about an hour Raeney and McFarland's boat touched the foot of the steps. Mc was introduced to Pontoon in due form, and then taking us [to] one side asked in a low tone, "What kind of a girl is this that you are throwing on to me?" "She belongs to the Church," we gravely replied, "and if you don't look out will entertain you with some very solemn Methodist hymns." "She's the gal for me," exclaimed Mc with a merry twinkle in his black eye.

Thursday, Feb. 15th. We left the steamer early this morning as we were anxious to reach the top of the Corcovado, before the sun became too hot. We took a hack and rode to the gardens, leaving the hack to wait our return we ascended the mountain on foot. The entire top of the mountain is perfectly flat and is a favorite resort for picnic parties, a great many of which are held during the summer season. The view from the top of the mountain is perfectly magnificent. Right at your feet lies the city, looking as antiquated and old fashioned as possible. Everything about it seemed perfectly lifeless. None of the energetic wide awake spirit of our American cities. It looked more like a grave yard than a large city full of living people. Beyond the city for more than fifty miles a stretch of country was spread out before you. All the hills and valleys were so quiet and still. Large coffee plantations could be seen in the dim distance and with a glass the slaves at work in the fields. Once and a while a pack mule with a large load on his back could be seen coming down one of the mountain paths. The sight, beautiful at first, soon became wearisome from its extreme monotony. Turning round the great ocean spread out before us, and she seemed like an old friend again. Far in the distance could be seen half a dozen clipper ships on their way to and from Cal. Almost at the mouth of the harbor cruised a large Spanish man-of-war watching like an eager bird of prey for the coming out of a poor little Chilian bark. She had been waiting for her three months, and the Captain, whom we met at Capt Baldwin's store, told us that she might wait three more. We had an invitation to dinner on board the *Shamokin* at five o'clock today, and must therefore stir about and see what there is to be seen in a very short time. On this table land are some large artificial lakes, which supply the entire city with pure sweet water. These lakes are constructed in the midst of a dense forest. These trees cool the atmosphere thereby condensing the vapor which falls in showers into the lakes. The water is carried to the city through an aqueduct which is the finest piece of work in the city. It was built under the supervision of Vasconcelius[10] and is an imitation of the Alcant[a]ra Aqueduct at Lisbon. It is carried to the city on arches which sweep high over the houses. We reached the steamer about 2 p.m. and found three or four boats from the *Shamokin* ready to carry the entire party of ladies over to the man-of-war on a visit. We waited and went over in Lieut McFarland's boat. The girls spent two or three hours examining the ship and seemed to be very much delighted with all they saw. We remained on board after the party had left. At the dinner table we found Miss B_____ and the young lady who admired brass buttons. Everything at the table went on very nicely until the young lady, whose contact with Rio water had not entirely destroyed her temperance principles, created a general laugh by filling her champagne glass half full of water. The poor girl blushed to the very roots of her hair, and the officer who sat next to her emptied the glass and refilled it with champagne at the same time telling her that champagne and water always made a person tight. This seemed to restore her equinimity to such an extent that she drank two full glasses, which had the tendency to make her quite lively and interesting. After dinner all the gentlemen except the officers who had invited the girls, retired to the deck and spent an hour or two in smoking and chatting. Some six of the ladies, with by express invitation of Mr. Mercer [went] to call on the acting American Consul and his wife who reside in the little town of "Sebastian"[11] opposite Rio on the other side of the bay. We asked Miss A____ on her return what kind of a time she had? "Not very pleasant," she replied, "the Consul's [wife] was very cold and stiff in her manner toward us and seemed to think that we were a lot of marriageable stock fit only for anybody's pickings. I wish that I had not gone," said the poor girl, the tears coming into her eyes.[12] "Why did you not go with the party to[o] Pontoon?" we asked of that young lady, who at that moment made her appearance. "I suppose he didn't think I was good looking enough. Never mind I won't comb his old head for him any more."

Saturday, Feb. 17th. Rev. Mr. Simonton, an American Missionary, came on board, and gave the girls a very severe lecture on the necessity of conducting themselves with propriety for the balance of their lives. He was a solemn individual, and did not have a single pleasant word to say. He did not even shake hands with them, but after pronouncing the benediction made them a stiff bow and hurried away.[13]

The sympathy of Brazil is strongly in favor of the South, and the hatred of the first families towards a northern man is perfectly intense.[14] At the present time the city is full of the Sons of Chivalry, who talk loudly of what they are going to do with the North one of these bright mornings. The severe flogging which they have received seems only to make them more boastful of what they can do in the future. They will find that the ever lasting Yankee will be just as ready 10 years hence to take them in hand and give them a good sound spanking as they were five years ago. Brazil and the Argentine Republic are just now engaged in settling a nice little question with Paraguay for the possession of the river "Platte." Thus far the Allied Powers (as they are called) have had the worst of the bargain. Genl Lopes, the President of Paraguay, commands his troops in person. He is reputed to be a fine officer, and fully able to hold his own. The Brazilian Government has chartered two large American steamers to convey troops to the river. They will carry from 1000 to 1500 men. The result of the contest will be watched with the greatest interest and it is to be hoped that Brazil will get the worst of the fight.[15]

Sunday, Feb. 18th. This morning we took anchor and steamed down the harbor, passed the *Shamokin* and *Onward*. The officers waved their hats and cheered as we swept by, and the ladies waved their handkerchiefs in reply. The visit to Rio will long be remembered by every member of the party as one of the most pleasant chapters in the history of the Cruise of the *Continental*. Nothing of interest occurred on board, (except the birth of a son to Mrs. Boardman, the poor blind lady. Some may think it dreadful that she will never be able to look upon the face of her offspring, but we do not, for he is the very picture of his Father,) until we reached the mouth of the straits of Magalhaeas.[16]

Notes

1. From Shakespeare's *As You Like It*, Act V., scene 2.
2. Mercer was born in Illinois in 1839, so would have been about twenty-seven years old at the time of the voyage (*Northwest Livestock Journal* [Cheyenne, Wyoming], July 11, 1885).
3. This was Mr. Stevenson. He, his wife and newborn babe remained in California (Engle, p. 237). One of the girls later recalled that the little girl born on the trip had been named Continenttalla. (Ida May Barlow Pinkham to Charles Thorndyke, Seattle, 1926, in Sophie Frye Bass Library, Seattle Historical Society).
4. At this point in the journey, "Rod" was pleased to report to his readers: "It is with the greatest satisfaction that we are able to speak of the fine lady-like deportment of the young ladies thus far. In all their intercourse with the gentlemen, they have behaved with that true sense of womanly dignity which governs the actions of every lady who has been accustomed to good society" (*New York Times*, April 22, 1866, p. 5).
5. This would be the Corcovado, also known as the Hunchback.
6. At a later date Conant wrote: "One lady on the shady side of forty rose and said that, in her opinion, Mr. Mercer was right, and that they all ought to be thankful that they had such a good and faithful protector, and for her part, she would like to see how many of the ladies agreed with her, and were willing to carry out the wishes of Mr. Mercer. As soon as she sat down, Mr. Mercer put the question, and requested all who were in favor of what their friend had said to rise and remain standing while they were counted. The lady on the shady side of forty was the only one that rose" (*Social Voices*, April 23, 1868, p. 3).
7. In November of 1866 the emperor of Brazil liberated the national slaves, the profits of whose labors belonged to the crown (*American Annual Cyclopedia for 1866* [New York: D. Appleton and Co., 1873], p. 66). Then on the eleventh of May, in 1888, the Brazilian Parliament passed an unconditional emancipation act, which went into effect immediately. Thus, slavery was totally abolished in Brazil (W. E. Curtis, *Capitals of Spanish America* [New York: Harper and Bros., 1888], p. 706).
8. Luff – to sail into the wind. (*New College Standard Dictionary* [New York: Funk and Wagnalls, 1947], 708).
9. The trees as identified by Conant were the crotem, plantain, mango, and orange (*New York Times*, May 6, 1866, p. 1).
10. This is the Carioca Aqueduct. Conant is referring to one of the viceroys of Portugal who administered the city, Luis de Vasconcellos (D. P. Kidder and J. C. Fletcher, *Brazil and the Brazilians* [Philadelphia: Childs and Peterson, 1857], p. 63).
11. Sebastian became a part of the city of Rio (E. Reclus, *The Earth and Its Inhabitants. South America* [New York: D. Appleton and Company, 1895], II, 191).
12. Harriet Stevens was not as upset. "Soon, however, we were obliged to leave. . .that we might meet an engagement at the American Consul's who resides at Sebastian. . . . After passing several pleasant hours we returned to the *Continental*" (Harriet Stevens, *Washington Standard* [Olympia], June 16, 1866, p. 1).
13. Miss Stevens said this about Simonton: "He gave us an admirable discourse on the moral dangers incident to so great a change of life as that which we had proposed to our selves. After services we were presented individually" (*ibid.*).
14. One historian suggests that some of these immigrants were from the former Confederate States of America and had come to Brazil to seek greater freedom (A. Curtis Wilgus, *The Development of Hispanic America* [New York: Farrar and Rinehart, 1941], p. 325).

15. When in 1862, Francisco Solano Lopez inherited the dictatorship of Paraguay and was proclaimed president for ten years, he decided his interests were concerned in the Brazilian interference in Uruguay. On November 12, 1862 war began and it soon proved to be one of the most bloody interstate conflicts that had been fought in South America. Before the war's end most of the Paraguayan population had been enlisted in the service. On April 1, 1870, Lopez was captured by the Brazilian cavalry and was killed. Brazil, despite allied protests, took steps to annex Paraguay and to make that country pay the cost of the war, some $200,000,000. There were South American objections to all this, and in 1876, after considerable diplomatic bickering, Brazil withdrew her troops and left Paraguay to herself (*ibid.*, p. 470).

16. Conant was probably attempting the Portuguese spelling of Magellan, "Magalhães."

3

THROUGH THE STRAIT

F RIDAY, March 2d. We entered the Straits early this morning.[1] There
was a strong wind blowing at the time, and the air was cold and chilly.
Nothing was to be seen but a low barren shoal stretching from the base
of a promontory far into the Atlantic. The whole country has a cold and
most uninviting look. Our first stopping place was at Sandy Point which
is 120 miles from the mouth of the straits. The Chilian Government claim
possession of the straits and have established at this point a small Military
Post and at present hold undisputed sway over the straits. We came to anchor early in the afternoon and soon after a boat, with the Chilian flag
flying at its stern, was seen coming off from the shore. Opera glasses were
at once in requisition and we soon discovered that it contained an officer
in full dress. It proved to be the present Governor of the Post, Maximiano
Benemido. He was soon on board and received from Capt Winser the attentions due to an officer of his rank. After remaining on board for an hour,
he returned to the shore accompanied by some of the ladies and gentlemen. They were taken up to the residence of the Governor and passed a
pleasant hour in the reception room which was furnished in an elegant
and tasteful manner. On the walls we noticed some very fine engravings
of Grant, Dupont and Porter. The Governor seemed to be greatly interested
in the great struggle which has been going on in the States between freedom and slavery, and showed by his conversation that all his sympathies

were with the North. Connected with the Governor's residence was a nice little garden full of vegetables and flowers and the ladies were invited to pick as many of the latter as they chose.

During the afternoon large numbers of soldiers came on board, bringing with them large quantities of skins and feathers which they offered to exchange for whiskey, old clothes, or anything else that the passengers might have. In an instant the ladies were in a great state of excitement, and they brought everything that they could spare, and old clothes of all kinds and discriptions were exchanged for skins, feathers, eggs, &c. Whiskey bottles were in great demand, a number of which were filled with water and sold for the genuine article. One good Baptist brother, wishing to make a good thing and yet anxious to retain the good opinion which all seemed to have for his religious and temperance principles, hid one bottle of whiskey under his coat, and slyly beckoned one of the men into a corner. When he thought no one was looking he handed him the bottle, and took a large skin in exchange. Did no one witness the transaction? The Sunday School books would tell us that the eye of God witnessed it, but the particular eye that we shall speak of was in the head of Pontoon. With a loud laugh she called the attention of the company to the whiskey bottle which was sticking out of the man's pocket, and then turning to the unfortunate seller, she exclaimed, "Here is the man who is always talking to me about temperance, selling whiskey; do you think," addressing herself to him, "that you can pray for this man tonight that he may not be led into temptation?" The only excuse that Bro. P. could offer was, that if he did not sell it some body else would. In the evening the Governor came on board accompanied by his lady and son and took dinner with the Captain. After tea they came up into the main saloon where they were entertained for an hour or so with some fine music. At a late hour they returned to the shore highly delighted with their visit. Although this post has been in existence for nearly sixteen years, very little has been done in the way of improvement, and nature is here seen in her wildest state. On each side and running far inland are dense forests. Forty miles distant are seen a range of mountains looming high above the clouds. The scenery is grand and gloomy in its character and while it may excite your admiration, you can never fall in love with it. It stands before you like a cold proud beauty whom you can worship, but who utterly fails to excite the softer feelings of your nature.

Saturday, March 3d. This afternoon found us safely anchored at Port Gallent [Gallant] and soon a party of gentlemen went on shore. A little sign board was discovered on a small island, giving the names of the different vessels which have stopped here. Underneath them all we wrote the name of the *Continental,* and added that she was taking out one hundred ladies to gladden the hearts of the old bachelors of Washington Territory. Two of the gentlemen ascended one of the mountains in the vicinity and discovered some very fine specimens of quartz. There was every indication that these mountains contained large quantities of gold. One gentleman who has spent 15 years in the mines of California stated that where ever that quality of quartz existed, gold was sure to be found. Mr. Mercer afterwards went to the top of the mountain and planted the American flag. After his return to the ship, a meeting was held in the lower saloon which was attended by Mr. Mercer and Mother Carey's Chicken, at which it was unanimously resolved that the mountain should be called Mt. Mercer.

Sunday, March 4th. We came to anchor about two o'clock this afternoon at Port Tamer [Tamar] about 100 miles from Port Gallent. The scenery is of the same gloomy character that greeted us at Port Gallent. A party of ladies and gentlemen went on shore, and while the ladies strolled about gathering moss and shells, in company with Captain Winser we made our way up the mountain to a large piece of granite which grew perpendicular out of her side. The following inscription was written upon it:

> "H.B.M. Ship
> Salamorter   [Salamander?]
> Feb. 13th 1843"

The hulk of the ship worn and weather beaten lay upon the beach. Whether it was all that remained of the *Salamorter* could only be conjecture.

Large quantities of brick lay strewed about in every direction and when we were ready to return to the steamer, most of the ladies and gentlemen provided themselves with a brick to present to their friends who had remained on board. The Captain, not to be outdone by the younger members of the party, picked up two or three. The ladies were completely over come with our generosity and if they do not retain will always remember the gift. We passed Glazier Bay about 12 o'clock today. The land shoots in from the Straits for about a quarter of a mile. At the end of this little bay is a deep gorge completely filled with ice and snow. The gorge is so completely over shadowed by the mountains[2] that the sun never reaches it, and all the water that runs down from the mountain's side freezes at once.

Monday, March 5th. We did not reach Puerto Bueno till late in the evening and being completely shut in by high mountain walls, we could see nothing but the dark shaddows of their cold bleak sides upon the water. With an Indian Ugh of disgust we turned in.

Tuesday, March 6th. We did not get up this morning till Puerto Bueno was far in our rear. We reached Eden Harbor[3] about one o'clock. This is our last stopping place, & when compared with our former stopping places is a perfect garden of Eden. The sun was shining brightly at the time, and the air was as soft and balmy as in June. The harbor, if it can so be called, was alive with side wheel ducks.[4] This variety of bird is only found in Patagonia. Some writers entertain the idea that they are not able to fly. We watched them with some interest to see whether the theory would prove correct. They used their wings instead of their feet to carry them through the water. They rush along at great speed leaving behind them wakes precisely like those of a side wheel steamer. Then thoroughly frightened they struggle violently for a moment as if it required a great effort to get their wings out of the water, and then rise and fly for a short distance.[5] Some of the gentlemen secured a boat and taking a large party of ladies started for the shore. After sailing a short distance from the ship we entered a lovely little cove that seemed to be entirely shut in from the outward world. The water was clear as crystal and as we looked down into its bed completely covered with shining pebbles we could see fishes of all kinds and varieties swimming about. At the end of the cove we found a nice landing place, and the ladies were soon running about gathering flowers and evergreens. After dark the gentlemen built a large fire, and all the party gathered round it and had a high time, laughing and singing and cracking jokes, till the steam whistle recalled them to the ship.[6] Today at dinner Mrs. C_____ became very much disgusted with a piece of hard bread which she was trying to eat. Throwing it down upon the table she took her knife and commenced cutting it at the same time soliloquized thus to her self. "I paid twenty five dollars for this pair of teeth before I left L_____ but if I have got to keep on eating this stuff I shall not have a tooth left in my head by the time I reach Seattle."

Wednesday, March 7th. This is the last day that we shall spend in Patagonia and before night we shall be out upon the broad Pacific. This is the most delightful morning that we have experienced since entering the Straits. On the main shore rises Mt. Burney 6580 feet high,[7] its snow clad summit towering above the light fleecy clouds which are playing around her sides. On the same side a soft light mist hangs over the water and the reflections of the sun upon it gives it the appearance of an April shower, while on the opposite side far up upon the hills the sunlight was playing clear and cold reminding one of a New England autumn. Here comes old Miss Berry & Mrs. C_____ "Well! Miss Berry, don't you think that this is one of the grandest sights that you ever saw?" "Well! Mr. Conant," said she, "I do think that it is kinder nice, but what makes them big cracks in the rocks?" "Perhaps it was the effects of some great earthquake," we replied. "I was thinkin," said she, "of what the Bible says of the whole earth bein rent when Christ was crucified, and I didn't know but that these rocks might have been split then. Dont you think so?" "We cannot answer that question," we replied, "as we were not living here at the time." Miss B. walked away very much disgusted with the answer. Smith[8] and Sarmiento Channels are the most interesting portions of Patagonia. Their length 126 miles [9] and we have a constant succession of the wildest and most picturesque scenery. No where else except among the Alps can anything be found to compare with it. Little islands covered with moss, evergreens and flowers dot the water here and there. High cliffs and mountain headlands, whose steep walled sides come down almost to the water's edge come constantly into view, while a succession of little bays are often seen looking like havens of rest, so peaceful and so quiet. Often it seems as if some mighty earthquake had rent these mountains of rock assunder leaving between them a deep dark ravine. Often we see long gorges in these rocks filled with ice and snow, and to complete the picture, in the back ground far above the clouds rise the summits of the snow capped mountains. Here one can study nature in all her sublimity and grandeur and never grow weary. But who can picture out the scene so as to kindle in the minds of those who read the same enthusiasm that inspires the mind of those to see it? After leaving Sarmiento Channel the scenery is very beautiful, but its extreme sameness is very wearisome. It is a succession of large basins, and when in the centre of one of them, you seem to be completely locked in by high mountains of granite with no means of egress, but on nearing the end, a little channel is discovered leading into another basin of like character.

[Thursday, March 8th.] 3 p.m. We are now out in the Gulf of Penas and nothing is to be seen of land but the distant shore faintly delineated against the horizon.—Farewell Patagonia! The sight of thy rocky hills, deep ravines and snow clad mountains has given us a new and a deeper insight into the beautiful works of nature, and may it inspire our souls with a deeper and holier reverence for the name of him who planned it all for the pleasure and profit of men.

Sunday, March 11th. This morning when we turned out of our state room the sun was just peeping above the horizon setting the entire East in a blaze of golden light. Not a cloud was to be seen & a fresh breeze was blowing off from the shore. "This is perfectly delicious," we exclaimed, as we made our way to the hurricane deck. Here we found most of the ladies and judging from their smiling faces and joyous laugh, they must have felt in all its strength the inspiration of that beautiful morning. On our right rose bold and clear the Chilean shore, while to the left large numbers of sailing vessels were seen under full sail. One of these appeared to be a large steamer under full sail, heading in the same direction with ourselves. The distance was so great that it [was] impossible to make out her character. All eyes were fixed upon her and many of the young ladies hoped that it was an American man-of-war with plenty of young officers on board, who with hearts as large and pockets as deep as the Yankee boys that they had met at Rio, would see to it that they had a splendid time at Lota.

The officers finally succeeded at last in making her out to be a man-of-war. Although no sound could be heard, yet puffs of smoke seen at short intervals from his bows showed that he was firing signal guns for us to stop. As the port of Lota which was free from blockade, was only a few miles off, the Captain determined to try the speed of the *Continental,* and see if she could not reach the port first. The Yankee ship proved to be the faster sailor of the two, and but for a slight mistake, would have sent the proud Spaniard off with a flea in his ear. It seems that there are two ports here,—Lota and Coronel, which are divided from each other by a high headland stretching a little distance into the sea. We ran right by the little harbor of Lota and rushed with head long speed into the harbor of Coronel, which was a blockaded port. The shore was completely crowded with people, who were running about in the most excited manner. Many on horse back were riding down the steep bluffs to the shore with neck break speed. We all wondered what it meant and concluded that they must have heard of the *Continental* and were coming down to see what the Yankee girls were made of. We afterwards learned from Dr. Silver the American Consul at Lota that they thought us one of the men-of-war, daily expected in these waters to assist the Chilian Government in breaking up the Spanish blockade. We soon dropped anchor and the Captain went on shore, but only remained long enough to learn that he was in the wrong port and blockaded at that. We were soon steaming towards the entrance, but found it much easier to get in than to get out, for at the entrance we found the Spaniard with all his port holes open ready to give us a warm reception should we attempt to run past. As soon as we hove in sight she fired a blank shot across our bow and then as if enjoying the triumph of having got us into a tight corner, fired a heavy shotted shell along our star board quarter. As the shot whizzed by two of the ladies fainted. Some screamed and some wept, thinking that their last hour on earth had arrived. One of the ladies asked us if we thought that the Spaniards would take us all prisoners and carry us to Spain[10] there to eke out a miserable existence in dark and loathsome dungeons—There was no alternative, and the Yankee ship much against her will, was obliged to haul to, and soon a large boat, manned with a full crew, armed to the teeth, came long side, and a more villainous set of cut throats never sailed the seas. The young officer who came on board to see what we were and to whom we belonged, behaved in a very gentlemanly manner. After a long examination of the ship's papers he finally made up his mind as to our character, and that we were not in the interest of the Chilian Government. We received permission to go to Lota and coal, & for all necessary supplies.[11] As soon as the officer stepped into his boat the two steamers dipped their flags, and amid loud cheers and waving of handkerchiefs, we parted; we to go into Lota, and he in search of a less fortunate victim. Night has cast her sable mantle over the harbor, and we are just able to see the dim outlines of the shore through the darkness. No sound is heard but the low hoarse murmering of the waves as they dash against the shore, or the rippling of the water against the ship's side as she rocks gently to and fro. The ladies completely worn out with the day's excitements have gone to their state rooms, and we are sitting alone at the piano writing. Alone did we say? A fair haired girl leans over our shoulder and exclaims "We do not wish to be classed, Sir, as an emigrant." We had headed our *Times* letter "The Female Emigration Expedition." To gratify her, we drew a long black line across the objectional part and wrote over it, The Cruise of the *Continental*. She was very much delighted with the change and called us a good boy.

Monday, March 12th. This morning we went on shore and called on Dr Silver the American Consul. He is a native of Ohio, and a perfect gentleman. He lives in an elegant mansion, situated on one of the highest bluffs, which commands a splendid view of the ocean and the surrounding country. The grounds round the house are large and are elegantly laid out. It seems to be one perfect sea of flowers. He said that we were very fortunate in getting off as easily as we did; that he fully expected the Spaniard to take possession of the ship and send us all prisoners of war to a little island, about 25 miles off, where they kept their prisoners under a strong guard until they could send them to Spain. The Dr had some splendid segars, which he placed upon the table and invited us to help ourselves.

After smoking he brought out some fine native wine and we all drank to the future success of the *Continental* Virgins. The Dr said that he could wait no longer, but must go on board and see the girls. The girls did their best to please the great man, as they thought him. He was very polite and affable to all, and on leaving the ship invited the ladies one and all to visit his house and gardens, and always to make themselves perfectly at home.

Tuesday, March 13th. We took a ramble through Lota today. The Captain's boat landed us at Lota proper. It is situated in a little valley between two high bluffs. It is composed of one story houses. The streets are unpaved and utterly destitute of trees or any other form of vegetation. It is the perfect picture of squalid misery and wretchedness. It didn't take a great while to do this part of the town, and we soon started for the upper town. The lower village was a paradise compared to this one. It is composed of little huts built of pine boards without doors or windows. Three sides were generally closed, while the fourth was opened. A few stones placed in the middle of the hut served in place of a stove. The huts are generally full of smoke and it is almost impossible to distinguish objects inside. The owners of these huts are generally engaged in the fruit business and they have five or six large baskets filled with grapes, apples, pears and peaches just outside the heat. We took a peep into one of these huts, and as soon as we could see through the smoke, discovered two or three old hags seated on the bare ground with a dirty ragged old blanket thrown over their shoulders. When they saw a pair of Yankee eyes peeping into their den, they grinned from ear to ear, and the sight of their toothless gums did not tend to excite our admiration of their beauty and we respectfully declined their sign of invitation to enter and make ourselves at home. Every thing was very cheap before our arrival, but as soon as it was known that we were going to coal there, business rapidly increased, and prices rose alarmingly.

Wednesday, March 14th. Today we went over to the English Mission which is under the charge of the Rev. Allen W. Gardiner.[12] His house is situated on a bluff about half a mile back of the upper village. He lives in a long one story house built with particular reference to earthquakes. Mr. Gardiner belongs to one of the 1st families of England, and just before coming to Chili, graduated with high honors from Christ College, Oxford. He is a man that truly loves his work, and his highest ambition seems to be to make this mission successful. His wife was one of the most accomplished ladies we ever met. She was the daughter of an English Lord. We looked upon them both with feelings of admiration and reverence. When we left Mrs. G. told us that we must make their house our home as much as possible during our stay at Lota. We returned to the ship late in the evening and found it filled with Chilian officers. One of them who can not speak a word of English has fallen desperately in love with Pontoon. He made a sign for her to take a chair and sitting down in front of her, looked at her all evening, the most intense admiration depicted on his countenance. He was very wealthy and belonged to one of the 1st families of Chili. Pontoon has caught a beau worth having, and she will marry him if she studies her own interests. Many of these officers are well educated men, and can talk the English language with fluency.

Thursday, March 15th. We took a party over to Mr. Gardiner's today at Mrs. G.'s particular request. The table was an elegant one. There was some splendid wine on the table, to which Pontoon did ample justice. Mrs. G. had spoken to us the day before of a desire to secure a lady to assist in the Mission; one who would be willing to help a little in the management of the house, and be a companion to her. We recommended Pontoon, wishing to do the girl a favor. Today Mrs. G. watched the young lady very closely, and when she saw the amount of wine she could make way with her countenance fell. After dinner some of the party took a stroll down to the beach in search of shells leaving Mrs. Gardiner alone with Pontoon. On our way back to the ship we asked Pontoon what Mrs. G. had said to her. "Oh!" said Pontoon, "she was very anxious that I should come and live with her, but I told her that I had made up my mind to go on to San Francisco." An offer of marriage from her admirer awaited the arrival of Pontoon. She said that she would take the matter into consideration. We think that she means to flirt with him all she can, while the ship remains in port and then give him the slip. Most of the officers are working with the girls to induce them to remain in Chili and teach. One of them received an offer of $1000, to teach in a convent 15 miles in the interior. They have made some impression and there is no knowing but that we shall lose some of our party here.

Friday, March 16th. Last night we met with a mishap which came very near bringing this Journal to an abrupt close. We had taken our note book, into the lower saloon to write out the events of the day, and while passing the table on the port side, fell through one of the trap doors of the coal hole, which had been left open by mistake. As we suddenly disappeared from sight, the ladies screamed, and as we lay upon a heap of soft coal, we were much amused to hear their remarks. "Oh! Captain Winser, Mr. C_____ has fallen into the coal hole and broken his neck." "Oh! Mr. C_____ is killed! Mr. C_____ is killed," screamed two or three voices in chorus. One widow, we learned, wept. As soon as we recovered from the slight shock we received in falling, we looked up towards the opening and saw half a dozen anxious faces looking down. We were soon on our feet, and two or three strong pair of arms seized hold of us, and we were drawn out, almost as fast as we went in. When it was discovered that no damage was done, the girls gathered round and commencing laughing and asking all sorts of questions, "which one was it that we intended to commit suicide for?" If we would only tell them, they would instantly accept to prevent another such catastrophe. As that was making the matter a little too serious, and fearing that they might be a little to[o] willing, we refrained from making any answer. As we had accepted an invitation to take a horse back ride with Mr. Gardiner, we went on shore in the first boat. We found Mr. Gardiner at the landing, with two of his finest saddle horses. Passing through the upper town we rode down to the beach, and were soon in full gallop for Coronel. This beach is one and a half miles wide and three miles long, and is a favorite riding resort for the Lotians. Every pleasant day, large parties can be found here, racing their horses up and down the beach. Leaving the beach we struck the hills, and rode our horses slowly up a steep narrow road. There was just room enough for two to ride abreast. On one side of the road the ground rose abruptly 40 to 50 feet, while the other side overlooked a steep precipice. One false step of the horses would have thrown us hundreds of feet on the rocks below. On reaching the top of the hill we saw the stage coach coming at full speed, and we turned off into the country. The country had a wild desolate appearance. Little huts made of four sticks driven in the ground and covered with branches of trees served as the dwelling places of the native farmers. Their plan of farming was decidedly simple. They would make a hole in the ground, and putting the seed in, leave the crops to take care of themselves till harvest time. Soon after we had turned off into the country, we met the Miss Berminghams' and the purser who had been over to Coronel, on a horse back ride. In about an hour we were riding through the principal street of Coronel. The village was composed of one story log houses, covered with red tiles. The people both male and female were a shiftless dirty looking set. The women as well as the men, were sitting outside the doors of the houses sunning themselves and smoking their dirty clay pipes. There was nothing interesting in the village, and in about half an hour, we turned our horses' heads in direction of Lota. Mr. Gardiner said that it would be better, to take a round about road, and thus avoid the afternoon stage. We rode along for about an hour over a dreary sanded waste, giving as he thought ample time for the stage to get ahead of us, but hardly had we struck the hills, when a wild hallowing and cracking of whips made us suddenly look round, and there was the stage coming after us at full speed. "Give your horse the rein, Mr. C_____," exclaimed Mr. Gardiner. "It will never do to let the stage over take us, for it will make them shy over the precipice." It was an exciting ride down that steep mountain road, but our good steeds were sure footed, and needed no assistance from us to keep them in the road. When we reached the beach the stage was far in our rear. After a splendid ride across the hard beach, we entered the hills of Lota, and were soon at Mr. G.'s house, and found a hot supper waiting for us to which we did ample justice. After supper we returned to the steamer pretty well fatigued with our day's excursion. On going on board we found the main saloon filled with Chilian Officers.[13] There is a regiment stationed here, and we have promised some of the Officers to visit the barracks tomorrow. The girls do not think that these Officers are one half as nice as the Yankee boys at Rio, and they probably have their own reasons for thinking so. But the officers are excusable for Lota is a mean insignificant place, with no attractions to make it pleasant. If it had two or three large factories, the girls would probably entertain a higher opinion of it. As equestrians the Chilian Officers cannot be excelled, and any lady who can sit a horse well receives from them the deepest homage. Miss B_____ accepted an invitation from one of the officers to take a horse back ride today. The horse assigned to her was a very high spirited animal full of life and fire. As soon as the party reached the parade ground he commenced cutting up some of his antics, and everybody present expected to [see] her thrown. But she succeeded in keeping her seat, and managed him with admiral skill and finally succeeded in bringing him to term. As soon as he became quiet she dismounted and was at once surrounded by a large number of sympathizing officers, and seventeen of them offered her marriage on the spot. She declined them all wishing to take her chances in Washington Territory.

Saturday, March 17th. This being the great market day at Lota,[14] the ladies determined to go ashore and make some purchases. They had not had a chance to go shopping since leaving New York and were fairly aching for an opportunity. It seems that the dealers in fruits, vegetables and plain clothes, were expecting a visit from the *Continental* ladies, and were looking their best, and to judge from their looks of self satisfaction, were expecting to drive some sharp bargains with their fair customers. If they had any such thoughts, it was a clear indication that they had never before seen a Yankee girl. Neither party could speak the language of the other, and the only way a bargain could be made, was for the lady to select what she wanted, and place the amount she was willing to pay either on the counter or in the lap of the seller. During the progress of these bargains there was a great deal of nodding and shaking of heads and smattering of English and Chilian. But the Yankee girls could generally out nod and out talk the sellers, and seizing what they wanted threw down what they were willing to pay, marched off, leaving the seller gazing after them with an astonished and bewildered air. We left the ladies driving their sharp bargains, and joining another party who had just come up the hill from the ship, went over to the Consul's. We found that gentleman in his office and he received the party with great politeness. He ordered his servant to place some wine and cake upon the table, & invited us all to lunch with him. After lunch we went into his beautiful garden, and the party scattered in all directions. We soon found ourselves on the splendid beach at the foot of the garden, and sitting down on a large rock, allowed our thoughts to run back to our Brooklyn home. Old Mother Ocean was our companion, and the noise of her mighty waves, as they rolled in towards the beach, and then receded with a deep and solemn sound, was perfect music to our ears. A light pull of the ear awoke us from our dream. "Come Mr. C_____," laughed Miss L_____ "don't sit there moping on that rock as if you had lost your last friend. Come and help me find some pretty shells." Miss L_____ is a niece of Major Haskel, an a. de C. on Genl Fremont's staff, and is a very bright pretty young lady. We spent an hour hunting after shells. On our return to the ship, we stopped a moment to see the Consul who gave us an invitation to take breakfast with him Monday morning. When we reached the ship we found a large number of Chilian Officers on board as usual, but we were very much surprised as well as pleased to see quite a number of Chilian ladies among the party. We all danced and sung and played cards much to the disgust of Mr. Mercer, who looked on in grim silence. He did not dare to open his mouth for fearing of offending the Consul. We asked one of the ladies with whom we had the pleasure of dancing, how she liked the American ladies? "I do not much love them," said she, "they make our men too sick." She was very anxious to know if they were a fair specimen of our American ladies? We gave her quite a long account of American Society, at the conclusion of which she threw up her hands and exclaimed "If these can draw away the hearts of our men, what would not those of your prettiest ones do?" Lota is becoming a port of some importance, and before many years her question may be answered.

It was twelve o'clock before the party left and it was with the greatest pleasure that Mr. Mercer saw them over the ship's side.

Sunday, March 18th. This morning it commenced raining hard, and every lady wore a gloomy face. It was a great disappointment to them all not to be able to go over to the Chapel to hear Mr. Gardiner. That gentleman had given them a very kind invitation to be present. To please them we took a boat and went up to the mission to see if he would not come on board and see them. We reached the mission wet to the skin. Mrs. Gardiner said that it was a bad day for one not acclimated to the country to be out, and she made us put on a suit of Mr. Gardiner's clothes, while she sent ours out to be dried. When we made our appearance she took us in charge and looking us full in the face for a moment said, "Mr. C_____ how could you as a gentleman recommend that Miss H_____ to me? She is an ignorant coarse woman and utterly unfitted for the position I wanted her to occupy." "Why, Mrs. Gardiner," we replied, "she said that you were very anxious for her to remain with you." "Anxious!" said that good lady with a smile of contempt. "When I asked her what she could do, she said that she could teach school, sew, do house work &c. That she belonged to the Episcopal Church, and had been a teacher in the Sunday School for many years. But on examination I found that she did not understand the first rudiments of a common school education, and as for her Sunday School teaching, she could not tell me the first question in the catechism. When I told her that she would not answer, she went down on her knees and begged me to take her. You ought to be ashamed Mr. C_____ for ever thinking of sending such a creature to me." And the little lady stamped her foot impatiently upon the floor. We did not know what to say in reply, for it was all too true, and we knew it. So we made as handsome an apology as we could, which the good lady in the kindness of her heart accepted, and we were good friends once more. After dinner we returned to the ship, with out Mr. G. who was too unwell to be out. The girls were all sorry but Mr. Mercer was mad. He thought if Mr. Gardiner cared anything for the souls of the ladies, he would have come, even at the risk of his own health. Mr. M. invited the ladies into the saloon to hear him preach but they were so angry with what he said respecting Mr. G_____ that they all retired to their state rooms, and left him to preach to himself.

Monday, March 19th. This morning we went over and took breakfast with the Consul. Quite a large number of Officers and other gentlemen were present. After breakfast which lasted an hour, wine and cigars were placed upon the table, and the gentlemen drank, smoked and talked till after twelve o'clock. After leaving the Consul's we went over to the village, and there found our friend _____ _____ two thirds in the wind. Fearing that some thing serious might happen to him, we tried to induce him to go on board with us. We succeeded in getting him as far as the beach, when he stopped and insisted upon singing the star spangled banner. We indulged him, and then tried to induce him to get into the boat. He looked at us in a very solemn manner for a moment and then said, "Mr. C_____ we would just, hic, as soon live, hic, as die," and turning about marched back to the town. The Consul and some of the Chilian Officers sent word this morning that they would be happy to pay their respects to the ladies this evening, and some of them have been hard at work cleaning the main saloon and putting things to rights generally. They expect to have a grand time and those who have had situations as teachers offered them, think that their voyage has come to an end. When Mercer went on to New York he was accompanied by a gay and festive youth, who, knowing Mercer too well would not trust him with the commission of selecting for him a wife. He visited his Grandmother, somewhere in New York State. Near the residence of the old lady dwelt a young and buxom lass, in whose eyes the young man found favor, and after a short courtship, with tears in her eyes she surrendered her heart into his keeping. They were married and went to New York to await the sailing of the *Continental.* While there she learned that while in Washington Territory, he had loved many young squaws neither wisely nor well. Becoming disgusted with him she turned her back upon him and returned to the land of her Fathers, leaving him with his wounded spirit to mourn his loss as best he might. As his simple and sole object was to secure a wife, he was in no wise disheartened by this mishap, but determined to make an assault upon the heart of one of the *Continental* party. The steamer had not left the harbor of New York before he selected one and commenced his siege. She was an honest good natured old maid of about 35, who seemed delighted with the idea of receiving any attentions from anything in the shape of a man.

Today she went to Mercer and told him that she had received an offer of marriage from Mr. Webster, and requested his advice and counsel. Instead of exposing the young man's character and telling her that he had a wife in the States he evaded the question, and told her that she had better wait until she reached Seattle, where she could obtain full particulars, well knowing at the time that he gave her this advice, she would never follow it. Seeing that she could get nothing out of Mercer, she determined to follow the inclination of her own heart, and at once went and threw herself into the young man's arms.

IS WASHINGTON TERRITORY IN DANGER?

THE MODERN ARK, THE MODERN NOAH, AND THE MODERN "WATERFALLS" THAT ARE ABOUT TO
DESCEND UPON WASHINGTON TERRITORY.

THE MODERN NOAH (*loq.*). "There, my dear young ladies, I think I see something."
CHORUS OF 400 UNMARRIED WOMEN. "Oh! please, Sir, is it a Man?"
THE MODERN NOAH. "No, bless ye! not a Man: it's a Gull."
MARY ANN (*aside.*) "Oh, dear! I wonder when we'll see a Man!"

A cartoon from *Harper's Weekly,* February 3, 1866, satirizing the Mercer party
(Washington State Historical Society)

Asa S. Mercer *(Museum of History and Industry, Seattle)*

The Territorial University in 1864 when Asa S. Mercer was president. The hand-carved columns are preserved on the present campus of the University of Washington *(Museum of History and Industry, Seattle)*

Tuesday, March 20th. Last night the Consul and a large party of Officers and gentlemen came on board. The Captain had a supper prepared for them in the lower saloon, from which the girls for whom the visit was intended, were excluded. Some of them amused themselves with looking over the railing of the large ventilator upon the party below. Mercer came up and seizing one of the young ladies by the arm rudely pulled her away from the railing, at the same time telling her not to make a fool of herself. "Mr. Mercer," she exclaimed, "I am a lady, and am not accustomed to being treated in that way by ruffians." "Your conduct, Madam in looking down upon that table, while the company were eating was most unlady like," said Mercer[.] "Oh! Mr. Mercer," she again exclaimed, "I hate you, yes, from the bottom of my heart, I hate you. And if my hatred could have killed you you would have been dead long ago." Mercer made no reply, but turned on his heel and walked away. The gentlemen soon came up and mixing with the ladies, were soon engaged in conversation, singing &c. They left about 12 o'clock, after promising to send a boat for the baggage of those of the party who wished to remain at Lota. This morning the boat came longside, with two of the Officers for the ladies and their trunks. Some of the ladies threw their arms round the girls and vowed that they should never go on shore with these men. Mr. Mercer stood in the gangway, with pistol in hand, his carrotty locks floating in the breeze. "No one," he hoarsely exclaimed, swinging his arm wildly in the air, "takes one of these girls from this ship except they passes over my dead body!" The girls cried and struggled with their friends, while the men in the boat swore great terrible oathes in Chilian. While this interesting excitement was at its height, the Captain came on board, and quietly ordered the 2d Mate to draw up the ladder. Turning to the girls he told them that they might go on shore the next day if they wished. The girls were comforted and smiling through their tears called the Captain a dear old Angel.

Wednesday, March 21st. The girls went to bed early last night in order to have happy dreams, of the delightful schools they expected to have when they left the ship. This morning they awoke to find themselves far out at sea. The Captain had taken anchor about 3 this morning.[15] The girls found that they had been sold, but they said nothing, in fact they were too sea sick to do or say much. After a stormy passage we entered the harbor of Talcuhuano [Talcahuano] on the afternoon of Thursday, March 22nd.[16] As soon as we came to anchor the Captain ordered his boat lowered, and invited a few of us to go on shore with him. As we were preparing to get into the boat, Mrs. Osborn came to us with a basket and requested us to bring it back full of grapes and tomatoes. After a row of about half a mile, we were landed at the end of a long pier. Talcuhuano is a most dismal dreary looking place. We will not speak too harshly as we saw it under the most unfavorable circumstances. None of the houses are more than one story high, and are divided from each other by little narrow courts which can hardly be called streets. In company with the Captain and the Doctor we made our way to the market. It was a large open yard completely surrounded by sheds. Under these sheds were seated large numbers of Indian women surrounded with large baskets of fruit and vegetables. We tried to play the old Indian woman from whom we bought the tomatoes a trick. We ordered two dozen and as fast as she put them into one end of the basket we took them out of the other. She caught us in the act, and not being able to see the point of the joke, prepared herself to pitch into us, and had it not been for the presence of the Captain and two or three more who came up at that moment, Roger Conant would not probably have been here to tell the tale. This port is a favorite resort for whalers, who wish to replenish their stores for a homeward voyage or another cruise. We found a large number of these whalers here. They gave us large numbers of whales teeth. They will serve to amuse the girls during the remainder of the voyage.

Notes

1. "At last the Straits of Magellan; there our progress was very slow as the ship traveled by day, the passage being so treacherous that it was thought wise to anchor every night" (Ida May Barlow Pinkham, p. 220).
2. ". . .which rise 13,000 feet" (Conant, *New York Times,* May 6, 1866, p. 1).
3. This place was sometimes referred to as Port Eden. "Navigators also find good shelter, abundance of fuel, pasturage and pure drinkable water in Port Eden south of the English Narrows, and in Puerto Bueno at the northern entrance to Smyth Strait" (Reclus, *The Earth and Its Inhabitants. South America,* II, 465-66).
4. Drawings of this species of duck may be found in Jean Delacour, *Waterfowl of the World* (London: Charles Scribners and Sons, 1954), p. 264.
5. To Conant these ducks seemed to fly very low for twenty to thirty yards, then drop suddenly down to the water *(Social Voices,* April 23, 1868, p. 3).
6. The ladies enjoyed the evening too. Harriet Stevens wrote: "Eden Harbor—Some gentlemen went on shore and added the charm of a great bonfire to the scene. Our California friend [Sniktaw] was among these. Next morning I heard a little lady assuring him that she had been in a state of great terror lest the Patagonians should find him of so agreeable a flavor that they would forget to extend the courtesy of a slice to his fellow passengers" (Harriet Stevens, *Puget Sound Daily* [Seattle], June 8, 1866, p. 1).
7. Harriet Stevens estimated the height of Mt. Burney as 5300 feet. She mentioned that she thought the hills and mountains on the shore of this passage had an average height greater than those of the Strait. *(ibid.).*

8. Sometimes spelled Smyth, but found spelled both ways on early maps.
9. Another description by a passenger: "On Monday, March 5th, we entered Smyth's Channel. The passage leading from the Straits of Magellan to the Island of Chiloe is divided into three channels, Smyth's, Messier and Sarmiento. At its widest part it measures six or seven miles, its narrowest only forty yards. By this time, however, it had become the general conviction that a labyrinth, of which Captain Winsor had not the clue, was an hypothesis contradictory of all the fundamental laws of the human mind" (Harriet Stevens, *Washington Standard* [Olympia], June 16, 1866, p. 1).
10. Conant must have thought this an expression of hope, in view of how he reported it to the *Times:* "I fear some of the fair ladies were disappointed at the result. A voyage to Spain would have been so romantic! But to the rest of us it was a great relief when our captor dipped her colors and allowed us to proceed to sea" *(New York Times,* May 6, 1866, p. 1).
11. Upon his arrival at Lota, Chile, Mercer was confronted with a copy of the *Times* in which there was news of trouble for him. His surprise is revealed in his letter to the *Times* dated March 19, 1866. Excerpts follow: "To the Editor...On my arrival here [Lota]...I find the following statement in your issue of Feb. 3d, 'A long argument was made Jan. 27th...in the case of Eliz. Thorne vs A. S. Mercer...' I never was more astonished in my life than by reading the news. In the first place I have paid out over $500 for the board of Mrs. Thorne and family....I fully expected to take her with me to the Territory, and gave her four and a half full fare tickets. But the great delay in New York cost me over $12,000 board money, and in consequence some one had to be left and she was one of them. There was one gentleman, Mr. Collins, who paid his fare, and one lady, Mrs. Balch. But six of all those on board paid their full fare, and none who were left, save those above mentioned, paid any part of their fare. I sent letters with the pilot from Sandy Hook, telling those who had paid how to proceed to get their money; and whether they did or did not receive reimbursement I have had no means thus far of determining....I deny any fraud or deception in the entire transaction. The enterprise is a success, and God sparing my life, it will be repeated next summer....I only ask justice at the hands of the public and those interested" (A. S. Mercer to editor, *New York Times,* May 6, 1866, p. 1).
12. "The English Missionary Society have established a large mission in Chili which is under the charge of the Rev. Allen W. Gardiner, and we can truly say that he is a man who loves his work. He belongs to one of the best English families and was educated at Oxford....He came to Lota five years ago, and although he has had obstacles to encounter, which would have discouraged the majority of men, he has overcome and trodden them all under his feet. He has a large mission school, opened daily, which is attended by nearly all the children in the settlement, without regard to their religious prejudices" (Conant, *New York Times,* June 10, 1866, p. 1).
13. Conant had more to say about the officers: "Ever since our arrival at this port, the *Continental* has been completely overrun, night and day, with Chilian officers. Some of them are very intelligent and well educated men. So intense has been their admiration of the ladies that every inducement has been held out to persuade them to remain in Chili. Offers of marriage, offers of schools at fabulous prices, and offers of positions as housekeepers flowed in in abundance and although some of the ladies have felt a little inclined to accept positions as teachers and housekeepers, yet it does not take long to convince them that South America is not a suitable residence for a young lady" *(ibid.).*

14. Conant further described some of the industries of Lota: "The principle trade of Lota consists of its coal. Previous to 1852, Señor Cossiner, a gentleman of fortune, visited the place, and became convinced of the existence of large quantities of coal. He purchased the entire property, and commenced working the mines. During the year he exported 5,348 tons, and his business gradually increased till the last year, when he exported 78,000 tons. The coal is bituminous, and of a very inferior quality. It varies in price from five dollars to 7.50 dollars per ton. There is also a fire brick manufactory which turns out 1,500,000 bricks annually" *(ibid.)*.

15. Captain Winsor and Mr. Mercer may have been forewarned by the letter which Mr. D. F. Sarmiento, minister from the Argentine Republic to the United States, wrote from Boston to the editor of *La Patria* at Valparaiso, Chile, and which was reported to have been printed in all the Chilean newspapers. After stating the advantages of an education for all the people, Mr. Sarmiento wrote: "Until that happy day arrives, welcome cordially the school mistresses from Boston, who will touch the coasts of Chili. When that day arrives another enterprise will be softly stranded on those resounding shores which will be a peaceful offering and an adequate and efficacious instrument for the realization of the idea—education for the whole people" (D. F. Sarmiento to editor *La Partia*, n.d., as translated and printed in *Boston Evening Transcript*, January 19, 1866, p. 1). The young Chilean officers did try to comply with Mr. Sarmiento's urging: "Honor and hospitality on their way to the holy women!...How sad it would be if that enterprise which sends the population of Massachusetts to fertilize Free States, should pass the coast of this whole continent...without meeting with a single country or nation which would desire to shorten its passage...and appropriate it for its own benefit. Six hundred North American school-mistresses in the Argentine Republic or in Chili, would repair in ten years the ravages of three centuries" *(ibid.)*.

16. The purser reported March 23 as the day the *Continental* entered Talcahuano. (*Alta California* [San Francisco], April 25, 1866, p. 1).

4

ON TO SAN FRANCISCO

FRIDAY, March 23rd. We took anchor this morning about 4 o'clock and attempted to run out in a dense fog. Fortunately both for the steamer and passengers, she had not proceeded far before she ran upon a sand bank. The Engineer crowded on all steam to make her go ahead, but with out avail, she would not budge a single inch. The air was so thick that it was impossible to see anything. In the afternoon a gentle breeze from the ocean scattered the fog and the sight that presented itself to the eye, struck a chill to every heart. Right in front of us rose up some of the most wicked looking breakers, that our eyes ever beheld, and had the steamer once got among them she would instantly have gone to pieces. At flood tide we floated off and instantly went to sea.

Tuesday, March 27th. The day after we left Talcuhuano Mr. Mercer commenced writing out some very suspicious looking papers. On Sunday he was so busy that he could not find time to preach one of Mr. Beecher's sermons. Yesterday he brought matters to a climax. The first lady he called into his state room was Mrs. Chase, and after stating that he had been to great expense in bringing out this party, told her that she must give him her note for two hundred ($250—) & fifty Dollars. She told him that he had promised [passage] to herself and two children for sixty dollars; that she had paid him that amount and would pay him no more. He said that he could not see what possible objection she could have to giving the note, as she would probably get a husband as soon as she reached Seattle, and he would pay the note. "Yes, Mr. Mercer," said she, "if I can find a man with white hairs, his pockets well lined with gold, one foot in the grave and the other just ready to go in, I might get married, but mind, none of his money shall ever find its way into your pocket." Mr. Mercer grew very red in the face and bit his lips in anger. "If you do not comply with my wishes," he exclaimed, "I will leave you without a cent in San Francisco." "Do it if you dare Sir," said she, sweeping out of the state room. With his next subject he was more successful. Poor old Aunt Berry was the victim. After stating what he wanted, he told her with a beaming smile that she would find a husband in Seattle, who would pay the note. "Oh! Mr. Mercer," she exclaimed, "do you think that there is any body up there who would be willing to marry me?" "Certainly," said he, "certainly. There is one nice old farmer who lives near me, who wants a wife, and he promised to take who ever I brought." "If that is the case," said she, "I will give you my note for any amount, if you will promise to recommend me to him." "I picked you out on purpose for him," said Mercer, at the same time handing her a note to sign, which she did with out reading it. After leaving him she went out on the hurricane deck, where we joined her. "Well, Miss Berry what did Mr. Mercer say to you?" we asked. "Oh! Mr. Conant," said she, "he did talk so nice. He told me that he already had a husband picked out for me, and won't it be nice to have a good home to go to as soon as I reach Seattle." "Yes," we replied, "If you are only sure of it." "Oh! I am sure of it," said she, "because Mr. Mercer said that he promised to marry who ever he would bring, and he told me that he had picked me out as the most suitable person in the party." "How much was the amount of your note?" we asked. She did not know. "How much did you gammon old Miss Berry out of?" we asked Mercer when we met him. "Only five hundred & fifty dollars," said he laughing. To make a long story short, some of them gave him their notes and some of them did not. Pontoon told him that she would see his red head in the bottom of hell before she would give him a red cent. The whole affair has created great excitement on ship board. Some of the ladies came to us and asked if Mercer would not be obliged to carry them through on the tickets which he gave them in New York. We were very sorry to be obliged to tell them that Mercer was not a responsible person, and as he had received no consideration, the tickets were not worth the paper they were written on.

Thursday, March 29th. In order to draw their attention away from the officers, Mr. Mercer has been trying to invent some new games and inducing the young ladies to play them. Among them were "Spiritual rappings," and guessing Proverbs.[1] The Continental Game being one of his own invention was a particular favorite with him. He would take a pack of cards, and writing a subject upon them, would distribute them face down to those engaged in the play. The first in order reverses the card rises and immediately proceeds to speak for five minutes on the subject which fate has assigned him. The play took amazingly with certain old maiden members of the party, but the young and gay couldn't see the joke, and flirted with the officers harder than ever.

Saturday, March 31st. Last night was the most beautiful that we have experienced since the commencement of the voyage. The night was so lovely that we determined to sit up and enjoy it. One of the girls who had been studying the almanac, came to us & asked if we intended to sit up and see the total eclipse of the moon. "That is what we are waiting to see," we smilingly replied. If we had been asked five minutes before if there was to be an eclipse of the moon that night, we should have answered no without the slightest hesitation. About 1 o'clock, the young lady, who declared her determination to sit up also and see the eclipse, exclaimed, "Mr. C! the moon is beginning to change color." We looked up and saw what appeared to be a little cloud of a dark brown color on the moon, while the moon was partially eclipsed, the eclipsed portion retained this color. But as soon as the eclipse became total, the whole surface of the moon changed to a light salmon color. This sudden change of hue created a great deal of surprise, and some of the girls who expected to see the moon disappear entirely from view, said it was not a bit nice, and that they did not believe that it was an eclipse. We were very much puzzled to account for this singular exhibition of celestial phenomena, and this morning took out our "Her[s]chel" to find some light upon it if possible. Her[s]chel gives an account of certain concurrent conditions capable of producing such an effect.[2]

Saturday, April 7th. Early this morning the outlines of land could be faintly seen against the horizon. We were approaching the Gallapogos [Gallapagos] Islands.[3] About 9 in the morning we came to anchor on the north side of Charles Island. These islands are of volcanic origin and do not present a very inviting appearance to the Immigrant. From the steamer not a tree could be seen, and the entire island appeared to be covered with long grass apparently dead. The Captain's boat was lowered, and we went on shore accompanied by a large party of ladies and gentlemen. The Island consisted of lava and volcanic products. It seemed to be utterly destitute of soil, yet we discovered quite a number of cactus plants and a few stunted trees. The gentlemen started for the interior of the Island in search of game,

but we preferred, not having a gun, to remain on the beach with the ladies, and assist them in searching for shells. Soon after the party had left
us, one of the ladies said, "Mr. Conant much as we admire you, for the
present, your room would be more acceptable than your company."[4] We
made a low bow, thanked her kindly for the hint, and left them. After a
walk of about 20 minutes we found ourself on a large flat rock. On turning
round the broad ocean was spread out before us and right at our feet was
the beach, and the ladies in their bare feet splashing about in the water,
and having apparently a splendid time. We watched them for a long time,
enjoying the scene hugely. When we saw them come up out of the water
and commence putting on their shoes and stockings, we descended from
our pleasant retreat, and rejoined them just as they had completed their
toilet. We asked them, if they had had a pleasant time during our absence
from them? Just as though we hadn't known what they had been doing
all the time. They replied that they had enjoyed themselves very much
& they one and all sincerely thanked us for having left them to themselves
for so long a time. We brought on board a large quantity of beautiful little
shells, but when the girls discovered what we had they made an assault
upon us, and in one minute and a half from the commencement of the
attack we did not have a single one left. Late in the afternoon we took anchor, and the engine having been repaired we sailed away. The last one
of the group was a large rock thrown up out of the water. It was almost
a perfect picture of an ancient Athenian temple. There were the heavy
columns, with deep wide archways between them. The entire rock was
clear and transparent as glass, and as the rays of the setting Sun were cast
full upon it, it appeared like one mass of glittering diamonds. It was one
of the most beautiful sights we ever saw, and we deeply regretted that the
10 knots an hour, which the steamer at the time was making, soon carried
us from its sight. It flashed upon us like a beautiful vision and was gone.[5]
We felt sorry that we were not the Captain, & that single want of over sight
on the part of the owners of the steamer prevented us from giving this
singular looking rock a thorough examination.

April 8th. The greatest flirt on ship board, at present, is Sniktaw. He
has gathered round him a group of six ladies of an uncertain age, and he
calls them his "constellation." He watches them with a jealous care, just
as though any of the young men cared to interfere, and he gathers them
together, at twilight, under his benevolent wings, even as a hen &c. One
of the group told us today that he was a fascinating compound of diffidence,
admiration, delicacy and abruptness.[6] Mr. Mercer pays no attention to this

flirtation. He probably thinks that he has no fears of Sniktaw, and in this opinion we agree with him. Mr. Mercer has entirely recovered from his own severe attack of love-sickness, and is now laying siege to the heart of Miss Annie Stevens [Stephens], an interesting lady of Irish descent and a most bigoted Catholic. She appears to be a willing victim, and is no doubt anxiously waiting for an offer of his heart and hand.

Thursday, April 12th. The flirtation between the officers and some of the ladies has gone so far that the Captain has felt compelled to interfere. The younger officers have begun to neglect their duties for the girls and the Captain has determined to put a stop to the whole thing. He has ordered the younger officers not to speak to or have anything to do with any of the ladies. Mercer is in his glory at last. There is one poor little man that rejoices over this change in the programme from the bottom of his heart. His wife is very pretty and a great flirt. The poor little wretch cannot bear to have her speak to a single man except himself. It is amusing to see her promenading the deck on the arm of one of the officers, and this perfect picture of misery, trotting after her right under her heels. This afternoon while sitting in the Captain's room smoking, some one knocked at the door, and at the command come in! Mr. Mercer appeared. "Captain," he exclaimed, "I discovered Hiss H____ talking to the 3d Engineer, and I ordered her to go to her state room and remain there 48 hours. Did I do right Sir?" "I will attend to it Mr. Mercer," replied the Captain. "I wish that confounded old Jackass would jump over board and drowned some dark night," muttered the Captain, after Mercer had left. Miss H____ did not go to her state [room] on Mercer's order, so back he came and the Captain, as she had broken one of his own orders, sent the 1st Officer to tell her to go to her room till he could see her. Her offense consisted in having offered to mend the coat of the Engineer. The Captain give her some good advice and released her from confinement.

Friday, April 13th. The Captain finds the enforcing of his order rather up hill business. The girls have denied his right to issue such an order, and have combined together to break it, and they seemed determined to flirt as much as they please. Last night the Captain told them that they must all be in their state rooms by ten o'clock. They did not go, and were determined not to go. It was a splendid little case of mutiny. The captain saw that his orders must be obeyed or all discipline would be at an end. Placing the 1st Officer at the head of the stairway leading from the upper into the lower saloon, to prevent them from coming up, he went up to one of them and taking her by the arm, marched her down into the lower saloon with out any ceremony. The balance at once saw the joke and scattered in all directions. It was a long and hard chase for the old man, but he finally captured the last bird, and peace once more reigned in Jerusalem. The girls seeing that the game was up went quietly to their state rooms.

Monday, April 16th. Yesterday during dinner time one of the girls and the 2d Mate drew a chalk line from the railing to the door on both sides of the main saloon and wrote underneath, "No subordinate officer allowed aft of this line."[7] When the Captain came and saw it he was in a perfect rage. He threatened to put all the girls under arrest and keep them in close confinement during the remainder of the voyage. He then put on a sweet smile and promised to forgive the one who did it and give her all the molasses she wanted for the rest of the voyage. This had the desired effect; the whole story came out, & poor Lockwood the 2d Mate is under arrest cursing the time when he became 2d Mate of the good steamship *Continental*.

Wednesday, April 18th. This afternoon the smoke of a steamer was seen in the distance. She rapidly approached and proved to be the *Golden Age* from Panama. She was a splendid looking steamer, and as she rose and fell with the waves, she seemed a perfect monarch of the seas. As she passed the passengers from both steamers cheered, and waved their hats and handkerchiefs. They must have crowded on all steam in order to pass us.

Tuesday, April 24th.[8] We are now passing through the Golden Gate, and before night the cruise of the *Continental* will come to an end. Most of the party however will proceed to Washington Territory, by some means or other. We shall follow them there and see what disposition is made of them. Coming round Black Point and passing Alcatraz Island we obtain a very fair view of the city. Our first view of this Western Metropolis is anything but favorable. The city seems to be built upon great banks of sand, and we should think that people residing upon these banks would roast alive some hot day. We came to anchor off Folsom St. Wharf, and we should judge from the looks of the crowd, and the way they looked at us, that it was the first time in their lives that they had ever seen a woman.[9]

Wednesday, April 25th.[10] This morning the ladies were taken from the ship and are now fairly settled at the International and Tremont [Fremont]. Fifteen have already broken away from the party, and more will probably follow.[11] Those who wish to taste the beauties of a territorial life, will probably be sent north in lumber vessels.[12]

Notes

1. Harriet Stevens mentioned these games, and another which she called "Throw Light Upon It." She did not describe it (Harriet Stevens, *Washington Standard* [Olympia], June 16, 1866, p. 1).
2. For further explanation of this eclipse see Sir John F. W. Herschel, *Outlines of Astronomy* (New York: P. F. Collier and Son, 1901 [1st ed., 1849]), XIX, 349-50.
3. "This group of islands is on or near the Equator, between longitude 89° and 92° W., 730 miles west of the coast of Ecuador, S.A., and consists of thirteen islands. . . . All are Volcanic and abound in lava" (*Gazetteer of the World* [Philadelphia: Lippincott, 1906], p. 692).
4. One girl, at least, was not responsive to his charms. She reminisced: "A newspaper correspondent, 'Rod,' of the *New York Times*,' who accompanied the expedition, paid open court to first one and then another of the fair sex, evidently with serious intentions each time, but the ardent wooer failed to make a permanent impression, his charmers suffered his devotions for a brief season and then gave him the cold shoulder" (Engle, pp. 231-32).
5. This may have been Genovesa or Tower Island.
6. Probably Harriet Stevens. Her description of Sniktaw was similar: "Our friend 'Sniktaw' has steadily increased in favor. There is a particular group. . . he calls the 'constellation.' As twilight approaches he may be seen as the central figure of that group. He is externally the ideal Californian. . .and I presume he may be considered one of her representative men. He stands before us very tall, broad-shouldered, sandy-complexioned, with a rough strong face, full of underlying good humor and energy. By birth a Virginian, though bred in Kentucky. He is a natural clear thinker, to which has been added the polish and accuracy of a liberal culture. From a student's life he passed directly to that of a miner, and fourteen years of almost entire seclusion from the society of ladies has made his manner toward them a rather fascinating compound of diffidence, admiration, delicacy and abruptness. . . . He has a passion for cold baths, clean linen and Graham bread. We are much indebted to him for the pleasure of the voyage. We have found him ever available for discussion, fun, declamation, and more substantial service" (Harriet Stevens, *Washington Standard* [Olympia], June 16, 1866, p. 1).
7. The plain spoken Miss S. helped draw the line (Engle, p. 233).
8. From *Social Voices*: "We are now rapidly approaching the Heads, and in less than an hour the good people of San Francisco will have an opportunity to see the long looked-for *Continental*, with her cargo of school-marms and housekeepers" (*Social Voices*, March 18, 1869, p. 3). A later entry added: "As we passed through the Golden Gate, all the ladies came on deck to obtain their first view of the promised land. Our first impressions of the great western metropolis as seen from the steamer, were anything but favorable; and as we looked upon the cold, bleek, barren-looking hills and sanded wastes, we could not keep back a longing for a sight once more of New England, with her beautiful hills and vallies and her magnificent forests. Not a tree could be seen, except here and there and that (to our unpracticed eye) had the appearance of an apple tree in the last stages of consumption. We were afterwards informed that they were scrub oaks, well named indeed" (*ibid.*, April 15, 1869, p. 2).

9. "As we neared the dock of the O.C. & M.S.S. Co., we could see the wharves completely lined with men anxious, no doubt, to obtain a view of the party, just as though the ladies were different from others of their sex. Great numbers came off to the steamer in boats, and offered large sums of money for the privilege of coming onboard; the Captain declined their offers" (*ibid.*). A San Franciscan reported the arrival. "The crowd finally became so oppressive that a strong force of police was necessary to keep them off the ship. They ought to have given the ladies a chance to recuperate a little after their long and tedious voyage, or at least a short time in which to make their toilets before they called on them. Mercer's ladies must have a poor opinion of the manners of the masculine portion of San Francisco" (*Alta California* [San Francisco], April 28, 1866, p. 2).

10. Under this date, Conant added in *Social Voices*: "We did not come on dock last night, and many anxious inquiries were made as to what Mr. Mercer intended to do. This morning when the steamer came to her berth the ladies were landed and at once conveyed to the International and Freemont House" (*Social Voices*, April 15, 1869, p. 2).

11. "May 1st. The crowd the past few days at the hotels has been very great. Gentlemen and ladies in search of help have kept Mr. Mercer in a constant state of excitement by the stories which they have poured into the ears of the ladies of the dismal condition of Washington Territory, and how foolish they would be to throw away their present opportunity of doing well here. About twenty of the ladies bent a listening ear, and bidding Mr. Mercer and the balance of the party good by, went away with their new friends. Today he made arrangements to send the party to the Sound on lumber vessels and this afternoon one-half of those who concluded to take their chances with him embarked on board the 'Scotland.' Last Saturday a rumor went floating round that Mr. Mercer, being unable to pay the board bills, intended to take the steamer for Victoria and desert the party. In a few minutes one half of the ladies were flying round in search of Mercer. They found him at the hotel, in his room, and gave him to understand that if he went on the steamer that afternoon he must take them with him. He did not go" (*ibid.*).

12. The merchandise brought to San Francisco by the *Continental* included "140 kegs of white lead, 30 kegs red lead, 1 cask lanterns, 9 cks packing, 10 bales rubber, 2 bales brooms, 3 bales felt, 1 bale lamp wicks, 7 cs bolts, 12 bales shovels, 3 bales 9s, 12 trunks merchandise. From Rio de Janeiro, 400 bags coffee. Consignees, A. S. Mercer: California, Oregon and Mexican Steamship Company" (Purser's Report *Alta California* [San Francisco], April 25, 1866, p. 1).

THE EVELESS EDEN

※※※※※※※※※※※※※※※※※※※※※※※※※※※※※※※※※※

TUESDAY, May 29th. We left the good bark *Huntsville*[1] this morning, and took the plunger *Maria*, Humbolt Jack, Captain, for Seattle. The day was beautiful and we had a delightful sail of 15 miles. We cannot say much of the country through which we have passed since entering the waters of Puget Sound, for we have seen nothing, with the exception of here and there a little one horse settlement, but water & pine forests.[2] We reached Seattle at 5 in the afternoon, and went at once to the Occidental Hotel.[3] Cut out a clearing from a dense forest on a side hill, one mile long and a quarter of a mile wide. Put about 50 houses in this clearing;[4] divide the settlement into two streets, filled up with sawdust. Give the place 3 hotels, 5 boarding houses, and 17 grogshops and you have a fair idea of Seattle, the town which for months had been in every body's mouth. The haven of rest, to which these tired and travel worn maidens had looked to and sighed for. The Occidental set an excellent table and after a hearty supper, we took a stroll through the town to see what the people had to say. They had a free and easy way with them common to people in a new country, and it did not take a great while to become acquainted with both men and women. I don't see what Mercer meant by bringing all those women up here for, where there is nothing for them to do, was the general and in fact only remark that we heard. One man told us that Mercer was considered a wild scheming fellow and that he had started this expedition for the express purpose of making money out of it. The people were all opposed to it, and not knowing what to do with all the women, hearing that he had left New York with 700 had made arrangements with the Gov. of Oregon to ship 500 of them to that state. The people have warm and hospital hearts, and have thrown open their doors to these poor creatures and have promised them a home till they can find something to do.

Tuesday, June 5th. We have been here one week and two or three strange incidents have occurred. There were some men in the Territory who were foolish enough to take stock in Mercer's Company.[5] He was not at all particular as to the character of the men who held stock, and it mattered little to him into whose hands he placed the happiness and keeping of the deluded females, who were crazy enough to place themselves under his charge, with the promise of a future home, so long as he obtained their money. We can mention only a few. Among those who took stock in the company, and who, hearing of the arrival of the party, hastened to Seattle with the full expectation of receiving a wife from the hands of Mercer, and upon being indignantly refused by the girls who wouldn't even speak to them, went away vowing vengeance against Mercer for bringing women that wasn't on the marry. We give the names that they went by on the Sound, and as we call them over, me thinks we see the smile of incredulity on your lips. Gentle reader, the names are correct, strange as it may seem and into the hands of these men did Mercer intend to consign these women. Here are the names of five which will be sufficient: Humbolt Jack,[6] Lame Duck Bill, Whiskey Jim, White pine Joe, and Bob tailed and Yeke. There was a young man who owned a little farm up the White river twenty miles back from Seattle. He wrote home to his friends in Ohio that he had a nice little farm, well stocked, and all he wanted to make his life perfectly happy was a wife. His friends wrote back that there was a young woman living near them who would be willing to come out and marry him if he would pay the expense. Hearing that Mercer was going to the States he placed $300 — in his hands to bring out this lady. Mercer accepted the commission and promised to write the young lady as soon as he reached N.Y., so that she could at once make her arrangements for returning with him. But Mercer put the money in his own pocket, and never communicated with the young lady at all. It so happened that another lady of the same name, but from another part of the country, a tailoress, who thinking from the great number of men in the territory that it would be an excellent place to drive her trade, came out as one of the party. The young man saw her name among the list of passengers published in the Seattle Daily; and with cheeks as red as a freshly blown piony and a heart throbbing with tender emotions and happiness, hastened down to Seattle to claim his prize. He arrived in town yesterday morning, and learning where the lady was stopping, made his way to the house. With trembling hand he gave a timid knock at the door and requested to see Miss K. He was shown into the best room, and soon a young lady with deep black eyes presented herself. As soon as she entered the youth rose and said, "Are you Miss K____?" "That is my name Sir," she replied. A broad grin over spread his face. Making a bow not over graceful in its movement, and throwing out his left leg behind to its full length, he said, "How are yer Mam?" "I am pretty well Sir," said the young lady with some surprise. "How do you do?"

"Middlin' only," replied the youth.

There was an awkward pause of a minute or two before the youth mustered courage enough to make known the object of his call. At last he made out to say, "I'm the feller what sent $300 by Mercer to bring you out for my wife. I suppose you are as willin' to get married this arternoon as any other time as I must be ter home by sundown to milk the cows and feed the pigs." "Sir," said the young lady, "you are either an impertinent fellow or else you are laboring under a delusion. You did not send $300 to bring me out. I paid my own passage. If you gave Mercer $300 to bring out a wife by the name of K____ you have been badly sold by him."

"Aint you Miss K____ of B____ Ohio?" asked the youth with a look of agony.

"No, Sir," said she, "I am from L____ N.Y." The youth looked on the floor for a moment as if engaged in deep thought. Looking up he exclaimed, "All I want is a wife and if you are willin' I would as soon take you as the other woman."

"I do not wish to marry Sir," said she with some asperity in her voice.

"Well," said the youth, with a kind of horse laugh, "if yer didn't come out to get married what the deuce did yer come out for?"

"To make pants, coats and vests," she laughingly replied, for she couldn't help pitying the poor wretch, "for such fellows as you are."

"Now if I were you," she continued, "I would go and have a reckoning with Mercer," and opening the door she was gone from his gaze.[7]

Today a man came rushing into Seattle, and requested us to give him an introduction to Mercer. As we had never seen the man before we had to laugh, but nevertheless gave him the desired introduction. He told Mercer that he had but half an hour to spend in town, as he must get back to his farm. He understood that Mercer had brought some women out there who wanted to get married, and he was glad to hear it as he had wanted a wife some time. That if the girls would be willing to place themselves under his charge for two or three days he would take two or three of them up to see his place and he felt sure that out of the number one could be found who would like to make it her home. Poor Man! Not one could be found who would go with him.

Friday, June 8th. We met Mercer near the Hotel this morning. He told us that Webster had married Miss J____⁸ the week before, and that he had sent for him to come down to Seattle to settle with him. Would we be kind enough to be present at the conversation. Mistaken wretch! to ask a reporter to witness a conversation of that character. We of course consented, for of course we would not allow any opportunity of gaining information respecting any member of the party to slip by. We went with him into the office of the only lawyer Seattle could boast of and shortly after Mr. Webster came in. Mr. Mercer opened the conversation by asking W. if his wife was well? Mr. W. replied that she was. Mercer then put on a severe look and said, "Mr. W. you have committed a great wrong, not only against the laws of your country, but to a young and confiding girl (she was only 35 and looked as if she could paddle her own canoe) by marrying her when you had another wife in the states. If you had waited, as I advised you to, till you reached home and obtained a divorce which would have cost you only Fifteen ($15) Dollars you would have been all right. But you have committed an act of bigamy and subjected yourself to be arrested and convicted for a criminal offense against a society," and a gleam of wicked triumph shot out of his eyes as he said these words. "But," he continued, "I will tell you what I will do. You promised to hold yourself responsible for the passage money of your Uncle, Aunt & their little boy; now if you will pay me $500 – down or give me a note on good security, I will say nothing about it, but if you do not pay me the money & give a note I will have you arrested and put in jail before sundown, and I will give you five minutes to make up your mind." W. said that he could not do anything without consulting his Father. He was very much frightened and did not know exactly what to do or say. Mercer stepped out of the room to see his lawyer, and W. turned to us and said, "Mr. C____ you are a lawyer, what would you advise me to do?" "You are welcome to our advice," we replied, "tell him when he comes in that you are going down town to see your business friend about the note. When you get out of sight mount your horse and make tracts for home. He is only trying to frighten you into paying for the passage of those people. He dare not prosecute you. He was well acquainted with all these facts before he sent for you; by bringing this matter before the courts he would make himself liable to arrest as an accessory to the act. But how," we continued, "did you prevail on old Bagley to marry you knowing as he did that you already had a wife in the States?" "He asked that question," replied Webster, "and asked if I had been divorced? I showed him a paper signed by my wife and myself agreeing to live apart. He said that was all the divorce he wanted, and married us without any more ado!" "Well!" said we, laughing, "you are both a healthy set of scoundrels and deserve to swing, but off with you." He did go and that is the last that we ever heard of him.

Saturday, June 9th. Today one of the younger girls having found a sighing swain to offer her a home appeared with him before Elder Bagley to be made one. The Elder asked her how old she was? "seventeen," said she. "You are not old enough according to the rules of this Territory to marry," said he seriously. "The law says that you must be over 18."[9] "But," he continued brightening up, "I guess we can fix it. Take off your shoes." She did so. He cut out two large pieces of paper to fit snugly in the shoes; wrote on them the figure 18, put them in the shoes. The girl put on her shoes and standing up was married over 18.[10] The old farmer which Mercer promised to Miss Berry did not come to time, and we very much doubt if he ever existed. She was considerably worked up about it, and told Mercer today that until he secured her a good husband willing to take care of her, he might whistle for his pay. Since coming to this country she has fastened her eye on a nice looking young man worth some property, who told us in confidence that he was soon going east to bring out a nice little wife in a Christian manner. Yesterday, Miss B. sent this young man a note stating that if he wished to marry her she would like to have him hurry up as she needed some one to take care of her. The young man sent a reply, calling her many names not found in the Dictionary, and closed by requesting her to visit a very hot place, which to say the least was a very ungentlemanly request on his part.

This morning an old back woodsman who could neither read or write, visited Seattle to inspect the party, and see if he could not secure a wife. He was introduced about 3 this afternoon to widow W. who brought out with her a Mother and three interesting sons, the neck of the youngest of whom we were on the point of wringing at least a dozen times during the voyage. At six he offered her his heart and hand; was accepted and at 9 o'clock, just one hour ago they were married. We do not know which of the two has been the most badly sold. For our own part we would not like to stand in either of their shoes. We take off our hat and make a low bow and bid the *Continental* & its party fare well for a season. If in after years anything of interest in their history should occur we will give the public the benefit of it, provided that in the meantime, we are not called upon to shake off this mortal coil. After a short tour through the Territory, during which we [saw] nothing but water, pine forests, and flat head Indians, we shook the dust from off our feet and took passage in the good ship *"Caroline Reed,"* Captain John Hinds, Master, for San Francisco. His wife & Mrs. Falk were passengers. After a pleasant passage of 10 days we landed once more in the city of sand hills and earthquakes. During our sojourn in the Territory, we met with only one baby, but we ran across hosts of young bachelors who would love to hear the sound "Pa Pa" from prattling lips.

The following marriages have already taken place:

Mrs. Mary J. Osborn to Mr. Atkins of Seattle.

Miss Ida Barlow to Mr. Pinkham of Seattle.

Miss Helen Stewart to Mr. Gassett of Seattle.

Miss Nina Manning to Mr. L. A. Treen, who came out on the *Continental*, but now of Olympia.

Miss Anna Stevens [Stephens] to Mr. A. S. Mercer, a wanderer who has no settled place of abode.

Mrs. Sarah Wakeman (widow with 3 children) to Mr. Washburn a farmer on the White river.

Miss Mary Grenold to Mr. McClellan of the White river country.

Miss Sarah M. Davidson to Mr. Baxter of Seattle.

Miss Maria Kinney [or Kenney] to Mr. Tingley, who came out on the *Continental*, now of Olympia.

Miss Almira Huntoon to Mr. Reichner [Ruoff] of Stockton, Cal.

Miss Mary Martin to Mr. Tallman of San Francisco. This lady is over 40 years of age, and the frisky youth who was over powered with her charms is about 25. He came out on the *Continental* as oiler.

Mrs. Horton to Mr. Buckley of Seattle. 70 years have already sighed their gentle breezes over her head. With one foot in the grave, and the other placed on the altar, she will probably pass the remainder of her days on earth, singing that good old song:

> "I am a gay and happy wife,
> For I've married a festive cuss;
> And I can recline for the rest of my life
> In his arms with out any fuss."

Miss Bianca Lawrence to Mr. ____ of San Josè.

More are spoken for, and as fast as they pass away we shall record them.

Mrs. Amada Chase to Mr. Harry Wiggins. Married in McGuire's Theatre by Laura Cappy. She is eight years the oldest. She was the lady who was going to marry an old man with one foot in the grave, and the other just ready to go in.

Miss Robinson to Mr. David Webster of the White river country.

Miss Sarah M. Staples to Mr. Edward Carroll all of S.F.

Mrs. John Lord to Mr. Elder all of Olympia W.T.

Miss Griffith to Mr. ____ all of Olympia W.T. This lady married a gentleman worth $100,000. She has done well.

Miss Flora A. Collins to Dr. Beardsley Surgeon U.S. Navy.[11]

A VALENTINE*

Sent to Dr. C. B. Brierly Feb. 14*th* 1867

You are a gay young medico,
So clap your hands in glee;
For you are considered the Prince of beaus,
By the girls you go to see.

I am a lovely little girl,
You, are all the world to me.
Oh, it puts my heart all in a twirl!
When you I chance to see.

I like a love sick little boy,
Who has petticoats on the brain;
I'll play with him like a little toy,
And chase him down the lane.

And when he gets tired, he can lay his head,
So nicely in my lap;
And dream that he is by Cupid led,
While he quietly takes his nap.

And we'll think ourselves under the grand old trees,
On the banks of a murmering stream;
Our faces fanned by the evening breeze,
Our souls lit up with the bright day dream.

But now I must no longer croak,
To your love no longer pander,
Excuse the words so loosely spoke,
By a goose unto a gander.

P.S. If the latter verse makes your spirit boil,
As an antidote take castor oil.

---

*This poem was recorded several pages beyond the last journal entry, at a later date.

Notes

1. "May 12th. This afternoon we saw the last lady of the party on board the barque 'Huntsville' and returned to the hotel just in time to see Mr. Mercer make over the piano of one of the ladies as security for the board of the party—and we guess it is all the pay the hotel proprietor will ever receive" (Conant, *Social Voices*, April 15, 1869, p. 2).

2. After three years' reflection upon his experiences, Conant was more flattering in his description of Puget Sound and Seattle than he had been in the journal. "May 28th.—We arrived this morning at the headwaters of Puget Sound. This beautiful body of water runs through nearly the entire length of the Territory, forming a large inland sea. Its banks, with here and there a little break for a small settlement, are completely lined with immense forests of pine. But we will not stop to give a description of the country, taking it for granted that its character is well known to our readers, but hasten on to Seattle, the haven of rest to which the tired and travel-worn maidens of the 'Continental' have sighed for months. The town is situated in a small clearing a quarter of a mile wide and about a mile long. The largest portion of the town is located on a side hill. Most of the private residences are built in the cottage style, and present a neat and tasty appearance. The Occidental Hotel stands in the center of the town, and is a model of its kind for a new country. After a nice dinner, fit for a king, we sallied forth to see the people. As is the case in all new settlements, they were glad to see one from the East. They are a noblehearted generous people, and opened wide their doors to receive the friendless strangers, giving them a home until they could find employment. Those who had families were provided with a house, rent free. No people could have done more. The young bachelors who had taken stock with Mercer were delighted when they heard of the arrival of the ladies, and at once commenced setting their houses in order to receive a bride, never once dreaming that the ladies would refuse to marry them" (*ibid.*).

3. "New Hotel.—By reference to our advertising columns, it will be seen that the new hotel, styled the Occidental, has just been opened in Seattle. . .and is fitted up in a style very creditable to them. . ." (*Puget Sound Herald* [Seattle], June 20, 1864, p. 2). An interesting description of the hotel was given by Sophie Frye Bass, whose mother was a contemporary of the Mercer Girls. "Occidental Avenue was almost Occidental waterway, a way of tides and logs and drift from Yesler's Mill, a way where Indians beached their canoes, and where crows dropped clams on the rocks to break the shells and swooped down in a rush before the watchful gulls could gobble them. Occidental Avenue came by the name easily for there was the Occidental Hotel right on it. . . . The Occidental Hotel, a white wooden building, I remember so well, for it was the first hotel I was ever in. From Second street, we had to cross a little bridge which led to the upper floor. . . .When I entered I gasped, for I had never seen such a long narrow hallway nor so many doors" (Sophie Frye Bass, *Pigtail Days In Old Seattle* [Portland, Ore.: Metropolitan Press, 1937], pp. 26, 27).

4. A year later, in 1867, Seattle was described as having "only 75 houses and 400 inhabitants" (*West Shore Magazine* for September as quoted in the *British Columbian* [New Westminster, B.C.], October 11, 1882, p. 3).

5. A copy of this contract as drawn up and signed by Mercer, with the names of the other signers omitted, follows: "I, A. S. Mercer, of Seattle, W.T., hereby agree to bring a suitable wife of good moral character and reputation, from the East to Seattle, on or before September, 1865, for each of the parties whose signatures are hereunto attached, they first paying me or my agent, the sum of three hundred dollars, with which to pay the passage of said ladies from the East and to compensate me for my trouble. (signed) A. S. Mercer, Seattle, W.T. March 1, 1865" (C. B. Bagley, p. 12).

6. In the first paragraph of this chapter, Conant mentions a Humbolt Jack as captain of the plunger *Maria*, a boat which plied the waters of Puget Sound.

7. At another time Conant wrote: "The young lady waited to hear no more, but rushed from the room, slamming the door after her. When we last saw him he was slowly paddling his canoe towards the mouth of the White river, and as the setting sun cast her last rays full upon his face, so sad and woe-begone in its expression, we could not help a feeling of pity for him" (*Social Voices*, April 15, 1869, p. 3).

8. This is an error. Webster married a Miss Robison or Robinson. Conant (p. 138) and Engle (p. 236) spelled it Robinson.

9. Other accounts of this differ. The following version agrees with that of Murray Morgan in *Skid Road*, and with others, and is more likely to be the correct one. "The joke was on Doctor Maynard. . . . At the time the doctor's love of fun nearly got the staid Daniel Bagley into trouble. A young couple who wished to get married sought the advice of Dr. Maynard, their difficulty being that the girl was not yet of the legal age of eighteen. That was a mere trifle to the versatile Maynard, who took two pieces of paper and wrote '18' on each and told the girl to put one of the papers in each of her shoes. He then went with the young people to the parson and assured Mr. Bagley that the girl was 'over 18.' Shortly after, when the irate parents descended upon Mr. Bagley he went indignantly to Dr. Maynard, who laughed heartily and explained what he had done. Seventy years later this young couple, Mr. and Mrs. Christopher Simmons of Olympia, recounted the details of their elopement, laughing heartily as they told them. Mr. Simmons being a nephew of Mrs. Maynard, knew of the good fellowship of the doctor" (Roberta Frye Watt, *4 Wagons West* [Portland, Ore.: Metropolitan Press, 1931], p. 351).

10. On January 20, 1866, the territorial legislature passed a law regulating marriages, and this law allowed males of twenty years of age or over and females of sixteen years of age or over to be married. If the "over 18" incident took place when Conant said it did, that is, after the arrival of the Mercer party, then the bit of chicanery on the part of Maynard was not necessary (See *Walla Walla Statesman*, March 2, 1866, p. 2, and M. S. Booth to Rev. John F. Damon in Bagley Collection of Letters, Misc. Folder, University of Washington Library).

11. An additional entry was found in the episode for the April, 1869, issue of *Social Voices.* "Since we gave our journal its last touches, we learn that all but two or three of the party are married, some happily, and some otherwise. One who formerly worked in one of the Lowell factories, recently married a gentleman in Olympia worth $100,000. Another, an old lady over seventy, married well. Poor old Aunt B___ has failed to find her farmer, and says that Mercer is a cheat and can whistle for the passage money" (*Social Voices*, April 15, 1869, p. 3).

APPENDIX A
The Passengers on the S.S. Continental

The landing at San Francisco marked the end of a three months' association of the members of Mercer's group with the S.S. *Continental.* Thirty-six persons, including five married men, their wives and children, two widows and the sons of one, eleven unmarried women, and five single men all remained in California. Though thirty-six might seem like a sizable loss to the Mercer party, it was little when compared to the loss of a group of women from Australia bound for Victoria, British Columbia:

> *The Seaman's Bride,* with about twenty females destined for this place [Victoria] put in at that port [San Francisco] for provisions and water the other day, and what did the young Yankees do? Alas! They captured the affections of the girls and induced them to remain there, while the vessel came on to this port without even a petticoat aboard to delight the eyes and cheer the palpitating hearts of the Victorians who were preparing to receive the young ladies with open arms.[1]

There is little evidence that Conant kept in close touch with the group of passengers settling in California, but about a few of them some information is available.

CHASE, Mrs., Eugene (her son), and Martha (her daughter). The Chase family came from Lowell, Massachusetts and initially went to Seattle. They later moved to California, where the mother became a spiritualist lecturer. In fact, she had spoken at several places while on Puget Sound.[2] She married Harry Wiggins.[3]

COLLINS, Miss Flora (Florence). She became the wife of a Dr. Beardsley, a surgeon in the United States Navy.[4]

GIFFORD, Leonard. Mrs. Engle listed him among those who settled in California but she may have been wrong, since a newspaper item listed him as one of the passengers disembarking from the barques *Vidette* and *Scotland* at Seattle.[5]

HUNTOON, Miss Almira. Dubbed "Pontoon" by Mr. McDougall, second mate of the *Continental*, she was a tailoress from Orange, Massachusetts, the eleventh child of James Huntoon by his second wife, Abigail Whipple.[6] Almira settled in Stockton, California, and, on January 2, 1867 in San Francisco, she married Charles Ruoff from Stockton.[7] Conant must have been mistaken in recording the man's name as Reichner, as the family genealogy as well as the newspaper account of the wedding gave Almira's married name as Ruoff.

LAWRENCE, Miss Bianca (Bina). She married a man from San Jose, California, his name unknown at this writing.[8]

MARTIN, Miss Mary (Molly). She married an oiler on the *Continental*, a Mr. Tallman. He was twenty-five, and she was over forty.[9]

SNIKTAW (William F. Watkins). Sniktaw did not resume his journalistic career for a year after his return to California. Immediately upon his arrival home, he filed suit and won his case against Mercer, in a San Francisco court. The jury awarded him possession of certain personal property and furniture that Mercer had purchased with money lent him by the *Californian*.[10] Thus Sniktaw, whose real name was William F. Watkins, salvaged some of his personal fortune and was able to continue his travels, as a bachelor.

When Sniktaw took up journalism again he was welcomed by the California press:

> Sniktaw, this fuliginous (smoky or sooty) individual has, after an exile of several months turned up, to use the common expression, somewhere among the defiles of the Rocky Mountains. He is writing letters for the newspapers and as his lucubrations are extensively copied, he is as happy as a June bug after an evening meal. Sniktaw deserves to do well, being a man of ability and speaking like Demosthenes, with pebbles in his mouth.[11]

A newspaper in 1867 revealed that he was to become a lecturer,[12] and this may be what drew him to the Rocky Mountain country. A few years later he showed up again in Patagonia, from whence came two letters to the *Alta California*.[13] Finally in 1878, news arrived from Panama that he had died there on January 26 of that year.[14]

STAPLES, Miss Sarah. She married Edward Carroll of San Francisco.[15]

No definite information is available about the following members of the group who settled in California:

Atkinson, Miss Julia
Bermingham (Birmingham), Misses Bessie and Mary (sisters)
Buckminster, Mrs. (a widow)
Guthrie, Miss Julia
Lewis, Tom and Dick (brothers)
Miller, Miss Annie
Peterson, Mr. and Mrs., and their three children
Rhodes, Mr. and Mrs., and baby
Spalding (Spaulding), Mr. and Mrs.
Stevenson, Mr. and Mrs., and newborn baby
Warren, Mrs. (a widow), and her two sons
Weeks, Mr. and Mrs., and baby
Weir (Wier), Miss Agnes[16]

There is more information about those passengers on the *Continental* who continued their journey to the Sound. The greater interest in Washington Territory may be attributed to the fact that the project originated there, and local pride in the results helped give it a prominent place in the history of the region. This awareness has been reflected in a number of personal reminiscences left by several of the participants. Prominent among these were Harriet Stevens,[17] Ida May Barlow Pinkham,[18] Anna Peebles Brown,[19] and her sister Libbie Peebles MacIntosh,[20] Anna Robinson (Robison) Webster,[21] and the oft-quoted Flora Pearson Engle.[22] The first two and the last are frequently referred to in the editorial annotations. Mrs. Engle's passenger list[23] has served as a good point of departure in compiling the data in this list, which is a composite of many lists and of innumerable fragments gleaned from widely scattered sources. Although it may be the most extensive to date, it is not complete, and variations and uncertainties in first names, in spellings and even in sex, have not been fully reconciled.

BACON, Misses Carrie and E. The purser's report listed these two women as passengers,[24] and C. B. Bagley's list included them,[25] but neither Conant nor Mrs. Engle made any mention of them. A Miss Bacon became a teacher in Seattle and lived at Third and Union.[26]

BARLOW, Miss Ida May. She was born on March 14, 1846 in New York City, and it was while she was attending boarding school in that city that she first began to dream of going west. She heard Mr. Mercer lecture on his colonization plan and then and there decided to go west to teach. Her twentieth birthday was celebrated while the *Continental* was at Lota, Chile. Her own account of arrival on the Sound reads:

> Later in the day we took a small boat into Seattle. Many of the three hundred inhabitants were there to see the new arrivals. Conspicuous were the young gallants of the town who came to see the girls of this much heralded expedition. One of the young men stepped forward and assisted me to land and accompanied me to the Occidental Hotel, a small two-story frame building, but at the time the best hotel in the city. This young man I afterward married. I would that I had the descriptive power to picture to you Seattle as I saw it that day. . . . You can see it if you erase from your mind the miles of docks and the imposing skyline that is the Seattle of today and imagine forest clad hills and a tiny village of straggling two story buildings; a white cupaloed building nestling in the hills above the city, the old University, and it seems to me that that white pillared building above the gallant little town expressed the true spirit of Seattle then and now, the high ideals and visions of those courageous early pioneers that hewed a mighty city out of the forest. That evening of our arrival most of the town people came down to the hotel to welcome the new arrivals and we later found out that the people were greatly relieved on perceiving our small numbers. . . . I found after my arrival that there was no school for me in Seattle, and Mr. Mercer offered me a school on Chambers Prairie, but I felt I would rather stay in Seattle, at least until my piano and other things arrived from New York.

Therefore, she started a private school which flourished for three months.[27]

According to Edmond S. Meany, Ida May Barlow and Albert Smith Pinkham were married on August 14, 1866. Their wedding was a gala occasion.

> Though there was no stringed orchestra and tall calla lilies and picture hatted bridesmaids, what a happy wedding it was! We were married in the Occidental Hotel and that evening all the young people in town came down to the hotel and made merry to the strains of the Seattle Band, and the Indians lined up outside the door and looked curiously in at the people and wondered at all the strange white people who made so much ado about a mere squaw.[28]

A few months after the happy event, they moved out in the wilderness on Fourth Avenue between Pike and Union. They lived there for a number of years until they built a home on Lake Union. "Although I did nothing in a big way to forward the growth of the city of Seattle, having raised eleven children I feel that I did it in a small way by helping the population that much."[29]

Mr. Pinkham was a merchant whose variety store was at the corner of Fountain and Elaine, opposite the Occidental Hotel.[30]

One of the limitations of frontier life was the lack of professional medical care. Two of the passengers on the *Continental* contributed their services to Seattle, Dr. Charles Barnard, dentist and surgeon, and Matthew A. Kelly, who became a pharmacist.

BARNARD, Dr. and Mrs. Charles. They took up residence in Seattle, and Dr. Barnard lost no time in hanging out his shingle and inserting the following announcement in the daily paper:

DR. CHARLES F. BARNARD
Dentist and Surgeon

Having established himself in Seattle, offers his professional services to those in need of them. Having devoted himself to the practice of Dentistry, in the city of Boston, for the last twenty years, except three years as surgeon in the U.S. Navy, and having the most approved dental instruments he feels confident in his ability to give satisfaction to those wishing his services. . . . Office at Kellogg's Drug Store, but when desired will visit parties at their residences. Office hours. . . [31]

Later, the doctor and his wife moved to Victoria, British Columbia.[32]

BARRY (Berry), Miss. Conant said Miss Barry never married,[33] but Mrs. Engle thought she had married a Seattle man by the name of Melson.[34]

BOARDMAN, Mr. and Mrs. They established themselves on a farm at Utsalady on Camano Island.[35] Mrs. Boardman was the blind lady who gave birth to a child during the voyage.

BOGART, Mr. and Mrs. James, and Charles (their son). This family chose Seattle as the site of their new home.[36] There Mr. Bogart became a butcher on Plummer Street at Eleventh Avenue.[37] In 1876 he was still a butcher, but his shop was at the corner of Ninth and Lane.[38] Some years later a directory lists him as the city jailer, residing on Ninth near Plummer.[39]

CONNOR, Miss Annie. She taught school in Olympia, where she met and married a Mr. Hartsuck (Hartsock) of that place. After his death she moved to Elma where she was still residing in 1915.[40]

DAVIDSON, Miss Sarah. She came from Lowell, Massachusetts and married D. K. Baxter.[41] A city directory for 1867 listed Mr. Baxter as a proprietor of the Exchange Saloon,[42] but in 1876 he had become a tanner and bootmaker, located at the corner of Third and Mill.[43] Some time during the next three years, he reverted to his earlier occupation of saloon keeper.[44] At this time he and his wife resided on Third near Marion.[45]

GRIFFIN, Miss Mary Anne. She wed Mr. Hartley, a farmer near Olympia. When he died she traded the farm for city property. She was dead by 1915.[46]

GRINOLD (Grenold, Grinnold), Mrs. (a widow), and Mary and Elvada (daughters). Mrs. Grinold married a farmer from the White River Valley, as did her elder daughter who married Frank McLellan of the same place. The younger daughter lived in Portland for some time. The mother and Mary were both dead by 1915.[47]

HILLS, H. O. From Oneida county, New York, Mr. Hills settled in Seattle. He became the father-in-law of J. J. McGilvra when his daughter Elizabeth Hills married the noted pioneer lawyer.[48] Other than that he lived with them at the corner of Cherry and Seventh streets, little is known of him.[49]

HORTON, Mrs. (a widow and the mother of Mrs. Wakeman). She married Ed Buckley,[50] who was a porter at the New England Hotel in Seattle.[51]

KELLY, Matthew A. A young orphan lad when he left Boston, "Matt" studied pharmacy in Olympia[52] and then opened the Pioneer Drug Store in Yesler's Block on Mill Street in Seattle. He became the local agent for "Mercer's Panacea," "the great medical discovery of Washington Territory, prepared by Dr. Thomas Mercer of Seattle," a brother of Asa. According to an advertisement of 1872, this "Tonic and Cathartic" was calculated to assist nature in overcoming disease more than anything yet offered, and "promotes digestion, as an appetiser has no equal. . .is particularly beneficial in eradicating from the system the effects of syphilis, no griping, no pain."[53] Kelly also sold another of Mercer's preparations, "The Ladies Balm." Matthew Kelly was still comparatively young when he passed away.[54]

KINNEY (Kenney), Miss Maria. One of the romances which probably had its beginnings on shipboard was that of Miss Kinney and Sam S. Tingley. After their marriage they lived for a while on a Skagit river farm.[55] In 1876, however, he was listed as a ship's carpenter, on Front Street between Pike and Pine, in Seattle. Mrs. Tingley was deceased by 1915.[56]

LORD, Mrs. (a widow), Clara (her daughter) and James (her son). This family went to Olympia where Mrs. Lord married a Mr. Elder, who may have been A. R. Elder, an attorney and probate judge. The daughter Clara accepted a school in Olympia, then married a Mr. Littlejohn. They lived in Tacoma where they were joined by Clara's mother after Mr. Elder's death. It is not clear what became of James.[57]

MANNING, Mr. and Mrs. A. A., Nina (their daughter), Edward and Anne Stevens (Mrs. Manning's son and daughter), all of South Boston. This family reached their destination on June 1, 1866, when the brigs *Tanner* and *Sheet Anchor* arrived in port carrying twenty of the Mercer party.[58] For the time being they tarried in Seattle, and on Christmas day of that year, Nina Manning and Lewis A. Treen, a fellow passenger, were married.[59] After a year in Seattle, where Treen had a shoemaking shop, he and his wife moved to Olympia.[60] There he opened a similar business and in 1870-71, he served in the territorial legislature. He was proud to have had a hand in securing the first clerkship ever given to a woman in the Washington legislative body, and that woman was Libbie Peebles.[61] Mr. and Mrs. Manning also moved to Olympia where he worked at his trade of shoemaking, possibly in partnership with his new son-in-law. His wife kept a private boarding home.[62] In 1879, the Mannings and the Treens were back in Seattle, the two men associated together in the shoemaking business.[63] Mrs. Treen died in 1905. The Treens had eight children born to them, and at least four of them were still living in 1916, in Seattle. They were Lewis A., Shirley M., Frank A., and Blanch Treen.[64]

MERCER, Asa Shinn. Mr. Mercer did not remain in Seattle very long after he had seen his charges safely to their destination. He appeared at a meeting at Yesler's Mill on a Wednesday evening, May 23, for the purpose of refuting the numerous stories that had been circulated "in the public prints and otherwise." In the audience were many of the fair emigrants, and their presence helped vindicate the young idealist's reputation. It seemed obvious to many in the audience that those who had been under his care placed the utmost confidence in him. According to one reporter's view, at least, the meeting adjourned with the best of good will toward Mercer and all concerned. He finished his talk with a statement to the effect that he had made good his representations to the government in spite of his enemies, which was some satisfaction for all the trouble he had in bringing some ninety persons who would benefit the country by their moral and mechanical labors. "That all he had promised them should be carried out to the letter, and with them he would stand or fall—so that the lying slanderers in the East, and the Klootchman lovers of this Territory might wallow in their filth, Fides et Justicia."[65]

On July 15, 1866, at the Methodist Protestant Church in Seattle, Asa Mercer and Annie E. Stephens of Baltimore, Maryland, were married by the Reverend Daniel Bagley, concluding another shipboard romance.[66]

Mercer continued to live an interesting and exciting life. However, he did not remain identified long with the territory which he had tried so earnestly to serve. In Oregon he devoted himself actively for several years to the development of trade relations with the Atlantic Coast and published several treatises of a promotional nature. After a period of seven years spent in Texas as a newspaper man, he went to Wyoming in 1883 and established the *Northwestern Livestock Journal.* One of his numerous publications was a book *The Banditti of the Plains,* which told the story of the cattlemen's invasion of Wyoming in 1892. Mercer died at the home of a daughter in Buffalo, Wyoming, on August 10, 1917. He was survived by three sons, two daughters, many grandchildren, and several great grandchildren.[67]

MERCER, Mr. and Mrs. W. Lewis (cousins of Asa). They lived in or near Seattle.[68]

OSBORNE, Mrs. Mary (a widow) and Eben (her son), natives of Lowell, Massachusetts[.] Mrs. Osborne's first husband was the son of a lighthouse keeper at Scituate, near Plymouth, and his family had lived there since Revolutionary War days.[69] After her arrival in the West, she taught at Tumwater on Chambers Prairie, near Olympia, and about a year later married Frank Atkins, a well-known Seattle pioneer. They had a son Frank R. Atkins who, in an interview in the *Seattle Post-Intelligencer* on January 7, 1955, said he was eighty-two years old. This would make his birthdate about 1873. Though he did not mention their names, this son said that his mother's sister, the sister's husband, and their son, were also members of the Mercer expedition.[70]

Eben Sumner Osborne, a son of Mary Osborne's first marriage, was born at Fall River, Massachusetts, May 10, 1856[71] and was just nine years old at the time of the voyage west. After accompanying his mother to their new home, he attended the University of Washington, studied for the law, became a member of the Seattle bar, and was later appointed city clerk, in which position he remained until 1885. His business career was entirely in Seattle, and among the positions he held were vice-president of the Washington Title Insurance Company, vice-president of the Seattle Trust Company, and manager and vice-president of Osborne, Tremper and Company, Inc.[72] On March 5, 1879, he married Carrie Meeker, the daughter of Ezra Meeker, noted western pioneer. They were the parents of four children, Eben Sumner, Jr., Ezra, Cora Osborne Brown, and Olive Osborne Jones. He died at his home in the Sherbrooke apartments, Seattle, after an illness of several weeks.[73]

PARKER, Mrs. (a widow). She was the sister of a prominent pioneer, Hiram Burnett. She married a man with the similar name of Burnell.[74]

PEARSON, Mrs. Daniel, D. O. (her son) and Flora (her daughter), all of Lowell, Massachusetts. Mrs. Pearson came west to join her husband and two daughters who had been with Mercer and his first party of emigrants in 1864. The family made its home on Whidbey Island, and Mrs. Pearson said, "This place is so beautiful I have only one step to take to get to heaven." She did not take that step until she had attained the age of seventy-one.[75]

D. O. Pearson was engaged at the time to Clara Stanwood of Lowell, Massachusetts, and two years later she came west to marry him. For several years he farmed on Whidbey Island, then moved to Camano Island. There, in 1877, he opened a store in the community he had named Stanwood in honor of his wife. At the time of his retirement from business, he was the oldest merchant (past eighty), and his store was the oldest store then in operation on the Sound.[76] A son, D. C. Pearson, succeeded him in this business but is now living in Seattle. In a recent communication to the editor, Pearson told of some aspects of the voyage which he remembered hearing from his father.

> The only information my father gave me was of his experience about the trip, and the difficulty in Mercer financing the cost of the trip. He said they left their home in Lowell, Mass., and went to New York for the ship sailing date, but the boat was not ready, and they were put up at a hotel several days. Mr. Mercer had agreed to pay these expenses, but at the sailing time the hotel owner put an attachment on all trunks and belongings, until proper financial arrangements were made, and this caused further delay. Father also told me that during the entire trip, meetings were being held by Mercer and his financial backers almost daily in wrangling over finances, as the number of passengers was so much less than expected, and was the final cause of the ship getting only so far as San Francisco. . . . Father never told me much of his first impressions of his new home, but he did give some facts about Grandfather Pearson [who was with the first Mercer group]. Each passenger was allowed a trunk, and as most of the male passengers were "lumberjacks," they had no use of a trunk, so Granddad got from six to ten men to allow him the use of their trunk, and filled them with boots and shoes, which he got in Boston at $2 and $3 per pair, and he brought them out here and peddled them at $10 and $20. The payments were made in hard money, so after the war, when paper money was worth about 53 cents, he sent the gold and silver east, and so made a handsome profit.[77]

Flora Pearson, a young lady of fourteen, kept a diary, and upon the basis of it, she later wrote an account of the momentous trip. Published in the *Washington Historical Quarterly* in October, 1915, it throws considerable light upon what happened during the three or four months' journey. Shortly after her arrival in the region, she became assistant lighthouse keeper at Admiralty Head. Then she married William B. Engle, a pioneer farmer. The ceremony took place at Victoria, B.C. After Mr. Engle's death in 1907, Mrs. Engle took rooms in Coupeville, Washington.[78] A son Carl died only recently.

PEEBLES, Misses Anna and Libbie (sisters), of New York. They made the journey for the expressed purpose of making a visit, seeing the country, and then returning to their home, but they found life on the Sound so pleasant they stayed on, secured employment, and later married men prominent in Seattle business affairs.[79]

Anna Peebles went on to Olympia a week after her arrival in Seattle, and was made very welcome by Mr. Barnes, the banker, and his wife, "who were most kind. I can't say the same of Mrs. Seluchius Garfielde who occupied herself in making slighting remarks about the Mercer party before me, assuming me to be one of them." Here one has an indication of a female passenger on the *Continental* disassociating herself from the Mercer party. Since the Peebles girls had paid their fares and had considered themselves to be merely passengers as they might have been on any other ship, they felt justified in denying Mercer's jurisdiction over their affairs.

Anna continued her narrative: "I started out as a deputy collector of internal revenue at $75 per month. I had to pick my way along the old Government road made for the telegraph."[80] On November 25, 1867, Amos Brown claimed her for his bride.[81] He was interested in various businesses and was listed as a capitalist in a Seattle directory.[82] The family at the time resided at 1110 Front Street, Seattle. Judging from a picture in a collection of the Washington Historical Society, it would seem that the lower half of the building and an adjoining addition, were used by Mr. Brown and his partner, Mr. Schmeigs, as a brewery, with the Browns making their home in the upper story.[83] This was the North Pacific Brewery, in which they held an interest, and porter, ale, and lager beer were the products advertised for sale.[84]

Libbie Peebles also went to Olympia where, with the assistance of Lewis A. Treen, she became the first woman clerk of the legislature.[85] She also taught school for at least four years in Lewis county at a settlement called Claquato, then the county seat. William Lemon, reminiscing, said that his son Millard, then a college graduate, thought this lady the best teacher he had ever had. The senior Mr. Lemon recalled that for four years the young Lemons all were pupils of Miss Peebles.[86] In 1871, Libbie married Angus MacIntosh, who had arrived on the coast in 1870.[87] Mr. MacIntosh became a very prominent business man as the following list of his enterprises will attest: he was the first abstractor in Seattle, after which he was treasurer of the Satsup Railroad Company, the Seattle Lumber Company, and the Safe Deposit Company, and was president of the Merchants' National Bank.[88] Mr. and Mrs. MacIntosh were the parents of two children,[89] and the family resided on the southeast corner of Third and University.[90] A son Kenneth served Washington well on the supreme court bench.[91]

The two Peebles sisters were agreed that pioneering on Puget Sound was never attended with the great sacrifices and hardships of many other places.[92]

PERRIGO, Mr. and Mrs. This couple lived in Seattle for a number of years. When Mrs. Perrigo died, he moved to Pilchuck where he married again.[93]

PETTYS (Pettis), Mr. and Mrs. Charles, and Charles, Jr. (their son). This family apparently dropped from sight, but Mrs. Engle knew enough about them to record that they all had died quite some time before 1915.[94]

READ, Frank. He lived at Wisconsin House in 1879 and spent some of his time as a gardener for H. L. Yesler.[95]

ROBINSON (Robison), Miss Sarah Anna. She married David Webster, a fellow passenger, on May 27, 1866 in Seattle, with the Reverend Daniel Bagley officiating.[96] Webster was a laborer,[97] a drayman,[98] and a teamster,[99] according to directory listings. He and his wife made their home at 219 Marion, west of Third.[100] He was dead by 1891. After many years had elapsed, Mrs. Webster was interviewed, and she told of their first winter in Seattle. She liked the country from the very first and thought it so beautiful she considered it a Paradise. "The first winter was very mild, and roses were in bloom. Some things were dear though. Potatoes were a dollar a bushel that winter, but smelts were plentiful at the foot of Pike Street and could be caught with a pin." The father of David and the father of the Peebles girls were cousins.[101]

SMITH, Miss Mary Jane. Of the four girls who went to Oregon she was the only one to marry, but whom she married is not known at this writing.[102]

STEPHENS (Stevens), Miss Annie E. She married Asa Mercer.

STEVENS, Miss Anne (a daughter of Mrs. Manning). She married a wealthy Mr. Gowey of Olympia and accompanied him to Japan where he died. Subsequently she married a Reverend Johnson (or Thompson) of California. This happened about 1910, and in 1915 she was still residing in that state.[103]

STEVENS, Edward (a son of Mrs. Manning). He became a telegraph operator in and near Olympia,[104] and then in 1882 he worked for Wells Fargo Express Company.[105] In 1915 he was living in Seattle.[106] For a while prior to that time he had been the agent for the Western Union Telegraph on the northwest corner of Main and Fifth in that city.[107] As Stevens and Treen approached the little village of Seattle in 1866, Stevens was said to have remarked that he would like to look upon the same scene fifty years later.[108] It would appear that he lived to do so, but unfortunately he left no record of his impressions.

STEVENS, Miss Mamie. She was a sister of Mrs. Asa Mercer and went to Portland, Oregon to live.[109]

STEVENS, Miss Harriet. Before going to Portland, Harriet lived in Olympia where she operated a private school for several years, until appointed to teach in an Olympia school.[110] Her account of the journey has been cited frequently in the notes to the journal.

STEWART, Miss Helen. She married Charles Gassett of Seattle, and little is known what became of them.[111]

TAYLOR, William. He left little record of his activities.[112]

TINGLEY, Sam. See entry for Miss M. Kinney.

TREEN, Lewis A. See entry under Mr. and Mrs. A. A. Manning.

WAKEMAN, Mrs. Sarah (a widow), Milner, Alfred, and Tudor (her sons). She and her family went to the White River country, after she married Andrew Washburn. The family lived for many years in that area, and the three sons all married in that section of King County.[113] Milner and Alfred eventually became farmers on their own. There is no record of Tudor.[114]

WEBSTER, David. See entry under Miss Sarah Robinson.

WILSON, Mr. and Mrs. John and John Henry (their son), from Massachusetts. Mr. Wilson lent Mr. Mercer money and received in partial payment a farm in the White River region. Although not of much value at the time the farm later became valuable, and it was then traded for city property. When hard times came, the family suffered severe losses. The son survived his parents and was living in Seattle in 1915.[115]

"Rod" Conant continued his association with the *New York Times* at least until the end of 1868. His dispatches, concerning a variety of subjects, appeared intermittently over this two-year period, approximately one a month, and usually a column in length.[116] It is most fitting that Roger Conant, himself, bid the readers adieu. Nearly three years had elapsed after the cruise of the *Continental* when Rod nostalgically penned these closing lines:

> Gentle readers, we thank you for your patience while we have told our story and we now make our bow, hoping that your cruise through life may be as pleasant and end as happily as the Cruise made by the good steamer *Continental*.
> —Roger Conant.[117]

Notes

1. *Colonist* (Victoria, B.C.), September 17, 1862, p. 3.
2. Engle, p. 236.
3. Conant, *Journal*, p. 138.
4. *Ibid.*
5. *Puget Sound Weekly* (Seattle), May 26, 1866, p. 4.
6. D. T. V. Huntoon, *Philip Hunton and His Descendants* (Canton, Mass.: Cambridge University Press, 1881), p. 59.
7. *Morning Call* (San Francisco), January 4, 1867, p. 3.
8. Conant, *Journal*, pp. 137-38.
9. Engle, p. 237. Conant, *Journal*, p. 137.
10. *Alta California* (San Francisco), May 4, 1866, p. 1.
11. *San Francisco Mercury*, November 17, 1867, p. 4.
12. *Alta California* (San Francisco), May 4, 1866, p. 1.
13. *Ibid.*, July 21, 1873, p. 1, and *ibid.*, September 13, 1873, p. 4.
14. *California Blue Book, 1907* (Sacramento: C. F. Curry, compiler, n.d.), p. 625.
15. Conant, *Journal*, pp. 137-38.
16. Engle, p. 237.
17. *Puget Sound Daily* (Seattle), May 29, 1866, p. 3; *ibid.*, May 30, 1866, p. 3; *ibid.*, May 31, 1866, p. 3; *ibid.*, June 5, 1866, p. 2; *ibid.*, June 6, 1866, p. 2; *ibid.*, June 7, 1866, p. 2; *ibid.*, June 8, 1866, p. 2. Also in *Washington Standard* (Olympia), June 9 and 16, 1866.
18. Ida May Barlow Pinkham, p. 221.
19. Interview with Mrs. Amos Brown, (*ca.* 1914), typescript in Sophie Frye Bass Library, Seattle Historical Society.
20. Interview with Mrs. Angus MacIntosh (*ca.* 1914), typescript in Sophie Frye Bass Library, Seattle Historical Society.
21. Interview with Mrs. David Webster (*ca.* 1914), typescript in Sophie Frye Bass Library in Seattle Historical Society.
22. Engle, p. 237.
23. *Ibid.*
24. *Alta California* (San Francisco), April 25, 1866, p. 1.
25. C. B. Bagley, p. 18.
26. *Directory of Seattle* (Seattle: R. D. Pitt, 1879), p. 38.
27. Ida May Barlow Pinkham, p. 220.
28. E. S. Meany, *Post-Intelligencer* (Seattle), May 15, 1919, p. 6.
29. Ida May Barlow Pinkham, p. 220.
30. *Directory of Seattle*, p. 62.
31. *Puget Sound Daily* (Seattle), May 26, 1866, p. 3.
32. Engle, p. 235.
33. Conant, *Journal*, p. 135.
34. Engle, p. 237.
35. *Ibid.*, p 235.
36. *Ibid.*
37. *Directory of Seattle*, p. 42.
38. *Business Directory for the City of Seattle for the Year 1876* (Seattle: Ward and Northrup, 1876), p. 46.
39. *Puget Sound Directory* (Olympia, Wash.: R. L. Polk, 1887), p. 219.
40. Engle, p. 237.

41. *Ibid.,* p. 236.
42. *Pacific Business Directory* (San Francisco: Langley, 1867), p. 329.
43. *Business Directory for the City of Seattle,* p. 75.
44. *Directory of Seattle,* p. 39.
45. *Puget Sound Business Directory* (Olympia, Wash.: Murphey and Harned, 1872-82), p. 24.
46. Engle, p. 237.
47. *Ibid.,* p. 236.
48. *Ibid.,* p. 237.
49. *Business Directory for the City of Seattle,* p. 75.
50. Conant, *Journal,* p. 137.
51. *Directory of Seattle City and King County* (Portland, Ore.: C. H. McIssac, 1885-86), p. 162.
52. Engle, p. 237.
53. *Puget Sound Business Directory,* n.p.
54. Engle, p. 237.
55. *Ibid.*
56. *Business Directory for the City of Seattle,* p. 74.
57. Engle, p. 237.
58. *Victoria Daily Chronicle,* June 6, 1866, p. 3; and *Puget Sound Daily* (Seattle), June 4, 1866, p. 2.
59. E. S. Meany, *Post-Intelligencer* (Seattle), April 8, 1916, p. 6
60. *Pacific Business Directory,* p. 329.
61. E. S. Meany, *Post-Intelligencer* (Seattle), April 8, 1916, p. 6.
62. Engle, p. 235.
63. *Directory of Seattle,* p. 68.
64. E. S. Meany, *Post-Intelligencer* (Seattle), April 8, 1916, p. 6.
65. *Puget Sound Weekly* (Seattle), May 26, 1866, p. 6.
66. C. B. Bagley, p. 10.
67. Charles W. Smith, "Asa Shinn Mercer, Pioneer in Western Publicity," *Pacific Northwest Quarterly,* XXVII (October, 1936), 347.
68. Engle, p. 236.
69. "Living Pioneers of Washington," *Post-Intelligencer* (Seattle), December 25, 1915.
70. Eleanor Bell, *Post-Intelligencer* (Seattle), January 7, 1955, p. 22.
71. *Wilbur Register,* November 30, 1939, n.p.
72. E. S. Meany, *Post-Intelligencer* (Seattle), December 25, 1915, p. 6.
73. Interview with E. S. Osborne, typescript in University of Washington Library, n.d.
74. Engle, p. 236.
75. *Ibid.,* p. 235.
76. Nina I. Kernighan, typed MS in Washington Historical Society Library, n.d.
77. D. C. Pearson to Lenna Deutsch, Seattle, May 22, 1957.
78. Engle, p. 235.
79. Brown interview.
80. *Ibid.*
81. G. E. Blankenship, *Thurston County Pioneer Reminiscences* (Olympia, Wash.: Mr. G. E. Blankenship, 1914), p. 388.
82. *Directory of Seattle City and King County,* p. 63.
83. Photo #28462 in Curtis Collection, Washington State Historical Society.
84. *Puget Sound Daily* (Seattle), May 1, 1866, p. 3.
85. Brown interview.

86. Blankenship, *Thurston County*, p. 184; and E. S. Meany, *Post-Intelligencer* (Seattle), April 8, 1916, p. 6.
87. *Magazine of Western History*, XII (June, 1890), 189-90.
88. *Directory of Seattle City and King County*, p. 118.
89. *Magazine of Western History*, XII (June, 1890), 189-90.
90. *Directory of Seattle City and King County*, p. 118.
91. *Magazine of Western History*, XII (June, 1890), 189-90.
92. Brown and MacIntosh interviews.
93. Engle, p. 235.
94. *Ibid.*
95. *Ibid.*, p. 237.
96. *Puget Sound Weekly* (Seattle), June 11, 1866.
97. *Directory of Seattle City and King County*, p. 162.
98. *Business Directory for the City of Seattle*, p. 75.
99. *Puget Sound Directory*, p. 352.
100. *Business Directory for the City of Seattle*, p. 75.
101. Webster interview.
102. Engle, p. 237.
103. *Ibid.*, p. 235.
104. *Ibid.*
105. J. C. Rathbun, *History of Thurston County* (Olympia, Wash.: J. C. Rathbun, 1895), p. 78.
106. Engle, p. 235.
107. *Puget Sound Directory*, p. 131.
108. E. S. Meany, *Post-Intelligencer* (Seattle), April 8, 1916, p. 6
109. Engle, p. 236.
110. *Ibid.*
111. *Ibid*, p. 237.
112. *Ibid.*
113. *Ibid.*, p. 236; *Puget Sound Directory*, p. 516.
114. *Puget Sound Directory*, p. 515.
115. Engle, p. 235.
116. Conant, *New York Times* on the following dates: in 1866–November 9, p. 2; in 1867–February 3, p. 1, February 26, p. 8, March 15, p. 1, April 3, p. 1, June 7, p. 2, August 14, p. 2, August 22, p. 8, October 10, p. 4, October 24, p. 2, November 3, p. 3, November 25, p. 5, December 12, p. 2, and December 26, p. 1; in 1868–January 12, p. 3, February 24, p. 2, March 5, p. 2, March 29, p. 10, May 1, p. 10, and June 3, p. 5.
117. *Social Voices*, April 15, 1869, p. 3.

APPENDIX B
Significant Documents

DOCUMENT 1. The letter of recommendation carried by Mercer, from Governor Pickering[1]

> Territory of Washington
> EXECUTIVE OFFICE
> Olympia, January 14th, 1865.

To all whom these presents shall come greeting

Know Ye, that I take great pleasure in stating that the bearer of this letter, the Honorable Asa Shinn Mercer, of Seattle, in King County, Washington Territory, is a Gentleman of the best standing in Society, is universally respected, as a man of honor, integrity, and moral worth.

Mr. Mercer will visit the Eastern and Western States, to work in the noble & good cause of aiding young women of respectability, to better their condition in life, by securing good homes in a new and exceedingly healthy & productive country.

Entire confidence may be placed in his statements and propositions, and in all his invitations to young women to accompany him to Washington Territory.

> Very respectfully yours &c &c
> William Pickering
> Governor of Washington Territory

DOCUMENT 2. Mercer's Circular[2]

Office of the New England Emigrant Aid
Company Boston September 8, 1863 [5]

Dear Sir: The steamship *Continental* will sail from New-York, direct for Puget Sound, about Sept. 20, to accommodate a party of ladies, composed of the orphan daughters and widows of slain Union soldiers, who propose emigrating to Washington Territory, on the Pacific Coast. Comfortable accommodations can be had for $150; other ladies at the very low rate of fare of $125 each.

Families will be received at the same rate, but that children in families are taken at half price; children under three years to go free.

We take the liberty of asking you to call the attention of any ladies who you think may wish to emigrate to the Pacific Coast to this opportunity. We have made arrangements with the most sedulous care for the comfort of the party. We know that there is a constant demand for the work of women in W.T. and that it is one of the most agreeable and promising points open for emigration. The citizens of the T. guarantee employment to all women of good character that will come.

Passage by any other route open to women is at least $350, and they are subject to every annoyance. This party will be accompanied by Mr. Mercer, the agent of the T., and the officers and crew of the ship have been selected under his direction. The ship has been fitted as a passenger ship by the United States Government, and was the finest vessel in their service for carrying passengers.

We do not advertise this emigration in the newspapers, because we only wish a class of emigrants who will improve the religion, morals and tone of society in the T. None but those who can furnish us with good references need apply. All kinds of manufacturers are very much needed, and can make money in the Territory, but this ship takes no men who are not accompanied by their families. 150 pounds of baggage are allowed each adult passenger. Each passenger is expected to find his or her own bedding. All persons wishing to join the expedition will please write to A. S. Mercer, at the Merchant's Hotel, Cortlandt St., N.Y. and receive full and definite instructions as to the day of sailing &c.

With great respect, your ob't servant
Edward E. Hale, Chairman Pacific
Committee N.E. Emigrant Aid Co.
A. S. Mercer Emigrant Agent for W.T.

DOCUMENT 3. Mercer to the *Seattle Gazette*[3]

Lowell, Mass., July 23, 1865.

Ed. Gazette: Through the Gazette and the Territorial papers generally, I wish to speak with the citizens of Puget Sound. The 19th of August I sailed from New York with upwards of three hundred war orphans — daughters of those brave, heroic sons of liberty, whose lives were given as offerings to appease the angry god of battle on many a plain and field in our recent war to perpetuate freedom and her institutions. I appeal to every true, warm-hearted family to open wide the door and share your home comforts with those whose lot is about to be cast in your midst. Let every neighborhood appoint a committee of a lady and a gentleman to meet us at Seattle upon the arrival of the ocean steamer carrying the party, with instructions to welcome to their homes as many of the company as they can furnish homes and employment for. Judging from the intelligence, patriotism and benevolence of the citizens of Washington Territory, I feel confident that a home will be found ready for each one of the three hundred young ladies I have induced to migrate to our new but interesting country. I can cheerfully vouch for the intelligence and moral character of all those persons accompanying me and take pleasure in saying that they will be a very desirable addition and help to the country.

Will the press generally aid us in getting these facts before the people. Very truly, A. S. Mercer.

DOCUMENT 4. Daniel Bagley to the public[4]

Seattle, Washington Territory
September 18, 1865

Dear Sir: Acting upon the information inclosed, a large and earnest meeting was held in this place on the 16th instant, to devise ways and means for the reception and care of the young ladies mentioned. Committees were appointed in the several towns and places of the territory for that purpose — the one at Seattle to act as executive committee, with Mrs. H. L. Yesler, president, on the part of the ladies, and W. E. Barnard, the gentlemen. Hon. C. C. Terry was chosen treasurer, and Daniel Bagley corresponding secretary; _____ _____ and yourself were appointed a committee for your part of the territory. The objects are, first: To provide homes and employment in families for as many as possible. Second: To secure places for a time for others until they can be permanently cared for; and third: To collect funds and articles to meet the immediate wants that must of necessity be pressing upon their arrival. It is thought a large number of blankets and of bed clothing of all kinds will be in demand. Prompt and efficient action must be had, or embarrassment and suffering be experienced by the orphans of our departed heroes. Humanity and patriotism alike, call upon us to make their condition as comfortable as possible. They may be expected here in a few days, hence something must be done without delay. We cannot now stop to question the propriety of Mr. Mercer's action. We trust it will result in good to the territory and all concerned. Please report at once how many we may send to your care, upon their arrival here. "To do good, and to communicate forget not, for with such sacrifices God is well pleased." Also, collect funds and articles and forward or report to me or the treasurer, Mr. Terry, of this place.

Daniel Bagley, Corresponding Secretary.

DOCUMENT 5. Edward Everett Hale to Frank B. Cooper, November 10, 1903[5]

39 Highland St.
Roxbury, Mass., November 16, 1903

My dear Sir:–

I have read with great interest the curious and valuable paper which you have sent me. I can hardly make you understand how curious it is to me, or how valuable.

In one of our Governor Andrew's messages, just after the War, he spoke of the "anxious, aimless women of Massachusetts." At that time it was almost impossible for women who were alone to emigrate to the Pacific. Men left us for every section of the world, but with enterprising or energetic young women it was much more difficult.

At this moment, in 1866, your Mr. Mercer heard of this expression of Governor Andrew and called upon him. I was at that time the vice president acting as President of the New England Emigrant Aid Society. Without knowing much about it, Andrew knew this, and he sent Merceir [*sic*] to me with a note of introduction. At that time Mercer was in the full hopes that General Grant's promise to him would be fulfilled, as he meant it should be. I think that we told him that we could send two hundred young women round the Cape to Seattle. On my part, I knew that there were that number of well-educated young women of the first character who would be glad to go. We put ourselves into communication through the enginery of our society with such people. If it were worth while I could look up any number of letters from such persons. But it very soon appeared that though Grant wanted to send out the Continental without any charge to Mercer, or to our Society the people who really managed the thing had no such intention. Poor Mr. Mercer had every annoyance put in his way, and every difficulty. It seemed to me that he maintained himself with great spirit through all these annoyances, and as you know, he succeeded in taking not two hundred, but still a sufficient number of ladies with him.

But here to me was the queer feature of the thing,—almost weird. As I remember it, I saw Mercer almost every day. I knew about the Janes and Marias and Huldahs who were going. Then suddenly, the curtain dropped. I have never heard a syllable from him, or from any of them since that time. It has seemed to me that the whole thing was like a dream. I came to be shy about talking about it till I received your letter.

You may be amused if I tell you one excellent speech of Mr. Mercer's. I carried him as my guest to hear the poet Lowell's Commemoration Ode, which marks to my mind the highest point yet reached by American poetry. Mercer sat at the banquet table between me and a New Englander, a class mate of mine,—a man with the sort of brag and swell which you western men ascribe to New Englanders. When it was told that a tenth part, say, of our students and graduates were in the War, this New Englander turned to Mr. Mercer and said, "Mr. Mercer, did your western colleges make so good a showing?" And Mr. Mercer said, "I was in Lafayette College at that time. The whole College volunteered as a regiment and the President went as their colonel." After this nobody bragged to him about our promptness.

Greatly obliged to you for your courtesy in answering my letter.

Truly yours, Edward E. Hale

DOCUMENT 6. Harriet Stevens to the Editor of the *Puget Sound Daily*[6]

Mr. Editor:—

I wonder if the good people of Washington Territory have any idea of the discouraging circumstances under which the handful of female immigrants landed upon your shores. My friend and myself arriving in San Francisco in good health and high courage, were surprised to find persons commissioned by friends in the East to seek us immediately on the arrival of the Continental, render us all the service of which we stood in need, and if our spirits were so crushed that we desired to return, secure passage for us. We had just finished what we considered the happiest three months of our lives, and it would be difficult to deject our state of mind. On reading letters from our friends, bewailing our hard fate, and beholding the actual presence of their agents, whom we had never before seen, but who evidently believed we had been led by misrepresentation to take passage with a party of ignorant, vicious people, from whose presence we should fly as from a pestilence. To our astonished vision they presented newspaper articles slandering Mr. Mercer and the whole party, and predicting for us the most disastrous and disagreeable fate. Mr. Mercer went on shore soon after our arrival, and being detained by business until the next day, found on his return the greater part of the ladies in tears. We were informed not only of the light in which we had been regarded in California, but there was no end of testimony as to the dismal character of Washington Territory; the ignorance, coarseness, and immorality of the people, and the impossibility of obtaining employment. It was added that the wrath of Washington Territory was such that Mr. Mercer's life was really in danger. That the most charitable construction of his character pointed to Stockton as altogether the most proper locality for such a visionary—that the people of Washington Territory utterly repudiated the whole thing, and considered themselves a decidedly abused people. The tone of the California press changed soon after our landing. One lady said in our presence: "Of course, no respectable woman came on the Continental;" but she had the delicacy and justice to entreat our pardon as soon as she learned that we were of the party. Another feminine, not quite so finely organized, assured us that we should never be respected on the Pacific coast because we came in that disreputable ship. There was no change in the clamor against Washington Territory. It daily increased. The friends of the ladies assured us in the most positive manner, that Puget Sound was the last place in the world for women, and offered all sorts of inducements to remain. Those who felt warranted by relationship positively vetoed leaving California. Some of the most agreeable and accomplished of the party were among those forbidden farther progress. But Washington Territory had been the land of our dreams for many months. Many of us could not be satisfied until we had seen it, and we determined to go on, although our hopes were greatly depressed by such a mass of testimony, which, strange to say, was rendered more emphatic by persons who either lived at the present time, or had formerly lived, on Puget Sound. I could not forget one thing—that was the decided and well known approbation of Governor Pickering in the early part of the undertaking. If Mr. Mercer was only a benevolent visionary, I could hardly suppose that to be the case with the Governor, and therefore the more Washington Territory was denounced, the more determined I became to learn the facts in the case for myself.

Shade of Falstaff! How this world is still "given to lying!" At the first sight of your beautiful little village my spirits began to revive. The fine structure occupying so grand a site, and devoted to education, is not, I reflected a bad commentary on the smaller houses below. As we approached nearer we beheld what was to us the most reassuring object in the world – the unclouded face of Mr. Mercer. We had feared that business would detain him in San Francisco. Considering how little reason we had to expect a welcome, Mrs. L. said, "if Mr. Mercer is not here I suspect they will put us in the pound." "I do not care," I replied, "if we can only go in a wheelbarrow, in true Pickwickean style," whereupon she consoled herself by a quotation from Othello.

I now believe that only the most conscientious determination not to awaken hopes that would not be realized has led Mr. Mercer to give impressions of Seattle so far below the truth. From the first I supposed it to be in a much more primitive condition than I find it. There is much more of comfort and refinement than I expected. As for the scenery, it would be paying Mr. Mercer a most extravigant [sic] compliment to say that he could over-rate its beauty in any attempt at description – only a poet of the first order could do that. But the one thing above all others with which I am satisfied, is the ample justification of Mr. Mercer's expedition, which I find in the facts stated publicly by Rev. Mr. Bagley. It is unfortunate that times have changed since the beginning of the enterprise, but surely that was no fault of Mr. Mercer's. For myself, I think the party is obtaining situations quite as rapidly as could be expected under the most favorable state of business affairs, and I believe that is the opinion which the party generally holds. I am happy to say, also, that they have experienced the same agreeable surprises in regard to the country and the people which I have expressed above. I begin to suspect that the natural influence[s] of the country are not only good for humans, but also for the brute creation. I have made the acquaintance of a family of kittens, aged six weeks, who possess an extent of territory above the eyes very unusual in kittens, and I must say that they justify this amplification of brow by the manner in which they watch the smoke as it goes up the chimney, putting out the paw, as if considering the *pro* and *con* of pouncing upon it. I am told, also, that the Postmaster has a very remarkable cow. During the voyage from San Francisco to Seattle I determined to go to Oregon; now, I think, if the citizens of Washington Territory should attempt to eject me from the country I should exhibit an amount of determination very detrimental to the matrimonial prospects of small women for all future time.

Very Respectfully,
Harriet F. Stevens.

Notes

1. From Charles W. Smith, "Asa Shinn Mercer, Pioneer in Western Publicity," *Pacific Northwest Quarterly*, XXVII (October, 1936), 355.
2. From *New York Times*, January 26, 1866, p. 2.
3. From C. B. Bagley, "The Mercer Immigration," *Oregon Historical Quarterly*, V (March, 1904), 1-24.
4. *Ibid.*
5. From Vernon Carstensen, "Two Letters Concerning the Mercer Girls," *Pacific Northwest Quarterly*, XXV (October, 1944), 343-47.
6. From *Puget Sound Daily*, June 2, 1866.

APPENDIX C
Problems and Rewards in Manuscript Research

Lenna A. Deutsch

Reprinted from *The Record,* 1962, pp. 45-50

When my husband, who was on sabbatical leave from Washington State University, planned to spend more time in the National Archives at Washington, D.C., to pursue historical research, I accompanied him. Not content to be idle, I volunteered to become his research assistant. Little did I realize that as a result of this experience I was to become ensnared in an historical project of my own. My task was to help him search for materials pertaining to the Inland Empire of the Pacific Northwest. This was absorbing work, made easier by early graduate training in scientific research, and by the many years I had lived in the area. It was rewarding to learn that I had a "good historical nose" and could sense the presence of pertinent information within a mass of papers with only a small clue to guide me.

As assistant I searched through containers of old documents, correspondence and the like, looking for anything pertaining to the Inland Empire. Some of the boxes had not been opened since they had been transferred to the Archives, others were [in] the original cannisters and had not been looked into for over a half-century. The dust rose when one of these older files was opened. In two different cannisters, I found the remains of a chocolate bar and a fig newton, long forgotten by an early-day departmental clerk who had been interrupted in his work and had failed to finish his snack. This should not be interpreted as a reflection upon archival housekeeping. These particular files had been in storage, and there had been insufficient staff to preprocess the great bulk of materials transferred from departmental files to the relatively new Archives building. As staff and time permitted, the papers were properly cleaned, flattened, repaired, and placed in standard containers.

There was such a plethora of northwest materials that our main problem was to make split-second decisions as to what was most important to have microfilmed then and what could be left for a later visit.

To many it seems strange that we should search at the opposite side of the continent for information on the Pacific Northwest. It is a fact that at no place in the east where we inquired were we turned away empty handed. Libraries and archives there were particularly lucrative sources for items we needed. Actually, other than in the region itself, the Atlantic seaboard offered more data than elsewhere. This may be attributed to two circumstances, namely: (1) Many New Englanders migrated westward and were quite articulate in their written accounts of their new homes; (2) Because of the trade and commerce between the two regions, promotional literature was likely to be more plentiful where it was initially distributed, rather than where it originated. Most obvious, Washington Territory was under federal jurisdiction, and many territorial records were deposited at the seat of government in the nation's capital.

After many weeks of working in the Records Divisions for Agriculture and The Interior, we went to the Department of Commerce Records Division for three days of work. It was there we met Mrs. Edward Poland who was doing research for a federal agency. When she overheard my husband speak of his interest in the Pacific Northwest, she told us of an early-day journal which she thought we should see. It concerned an account of the "Mercer Girls" of Seattle's early days and was in the possession of her husband's mother, Mrs. Helen Loud Poland, a niece of the diarist. We were assured by the younger Mrs. Poland that we would be welcome to see the journal. This fortunate coincidence brought us the good luck which could not have been anticipated and which may come to an historian but once in a lifetime.

Later that summer our quest took us to Cambridge, Massachusetts, to examine manuscript materials at the Houghton Library at Harvard University. We decided that on our homeward journey we would visit Loud Island and meet the elder Mrs. Poland and see the precious journal in her possession. We had been in correspondence with her, and she had graciously issued an invitation to us to visit her. Since there was no public transportation to Loud Island (named for her husband's family), she had suggested that we hire a lobster fisherman at Round Pound, Maine, to take us from the mainland. We engaged Mr. Bryant, a fisherman, who knew the island and put us ashore at a near sandy point a short distance from the lady's home. From there we strolled through a field of wild blueberries to the red-roofed house that had been barely visible through the trees. After serving us blueberry cake and coffee, our gracious hostess brought out the journal for our inspection. We had taken a Contoura Photocopy machine with us, hoping to be permitted to copy the document. However, to our disappointment, we learned the house had no electricity, so we were unable to use the machine. Because of the fire hazard, we urged Mrs. Poland to take the document with her the next time she visited her son in Washington, D.C. There she could ask the Library of Congress to microfilm it and keep the master copy for its files. She responded to this idea, and later that year we were notified that the work had been done.

Some time later we wrote asking permission to edit the journal for publication. Mrs. Poland replied that she was assured we were genuinely interested in it as a significant historical document and so very graciously granted our request. My husband was by then already engrossed in his own project, so he suggested that I assume the editing task. With his promise of help whenever I needed it and with considerable misgivings on my part as to my abilities for this type of assignment, I agreed to try.

The editing of an historical journal differs somewhat from other types of writing. The subject matter of the project is predetermined, and the editor must work within the framework of the subject as recorded by the chronicler. Research, therefore, begins within areas suggested by the journal's content. As a beginning, I transcribed the journal from the microfilm copy I had obtained from the Library of Congress.

The journal revealed a fascinating story but one that would have to be pursued further. In the year 1865, Asa Mercer of Seattle conceived a scheme of female emigration which he hoped would relieve the scarcity of women in the West and at the same time lessen the surplus of women in the New England states. He hoped to secure hundreds of women emigrants to take west with him and, toward this end, he conducted a publicity campaign in New York and New England. Roger Conant, a reporter for the *New York Times* and a young bachelor like Asa Mercer, became intrigued with the plan and kept in close touch with any new developments so he could report them to his paper. It was not surprising to find his name among the one hundred passengers who sailed for the West aboard the S.S. *Continental* on January 16, 1866. In addition to sending home reports from time to time under the byline "Rod," he kept a personal diary of happenings en route. It was this day-by-day account which constituted the nucleus for the book which I later edited under the title *Mercer's Belles—A Journal of a Reporter*.

The research had just begun with the journal. The real task lay ahead. To be sure I had experienced colossal good fortune in finding such a manuscript, but now materials must be found to supplement and illuminate the journal. I began at the Washington State University Library and checked the more obvious reference works, read items pertaining to female emigration in general and the Mercer female emigration in particular, and then perused the *New York Times* for the years 1865-1866. I wished to read "Rod's" dispatches as well as any other news stories leading up to the departure. This was most productive, yielding much information and many clues as to where further searches would be profitable. In a short time it became evident that much needed data would be found in widely scattered places. To visit them all would take more time and money than I could afford. Therefore, I found it necessary to take advantage of opportunities as they presented themselves.

Before I had exhausted all sources at Washington State University, I had an opportunity to visit several libraries elsewhere. One of these was the Bancroft Library at Berkeley, California. There I found copies, some in the original and others on microfilm, of early-day California newspapers. I had fun reading items about the Mercer expedition and the various editors' assessments of Mercer and his scheme and of the passengers who were brave enough to participate in it. I finally felt that I had exhausted the pertinent materials afforded by this library, but shortly after my return home I found a reference to a cartoon by a well-known cartoonist of that early period which ridiculed the Mercer Girls. It appeared that the only known copy of this was at the Bancroft Library. Fortunately, I had adequate identification so that the attendants at the library found it without difficulty and had it copied for me. It was used as an illustration in my book.

In research of this type, one uses all the research tools available. The *Reader's Guide to Periodical Literature,* the *Union List of Newspapers,* catalogs of collections, and various analytics of newspapers and collections were all utilized. However, lest one overlook pertinent material, one should not rely solely upon analytics. I recall, for instance, one British Columbia newspaper for which there was a very fine analytical guide. I had used it to good advantage, but, since I had some time left to work, I decided to read the paper carefully, page by page, for the pertinent months. I was rewarded with many additional items, some of a fringe nature but nonetheless important. Others I had failed to locate in the analytics because they were listed under headings not ordinarily associated with my subject.

The library of the Seattle Historical Society is not a large one but contains a fine collection of early-day photographs of the local scene, and a group of personal interviews obtained in 1914-1915. Several Mercer Girls were among those interviewed, and though many years had intervened, their recollections of the 1866 voyage were still vivid.

At the Seattle City Library I gleaned a great amount of biographical data about Conant and his family from the genealogical collection.

The University of Washington Library has a fine manuscript division with holdings rich in source material of the Puget Sound region. I found numerous references to Mercer and to members of his emigration party. As a matter of fact, one of Mercer's granddaughters had placed a collection of papers in that library for safe keeping. However, the librarian informed me that I would need her permission to examine them. When I sought such permission the granddaughter was reluctant to grant it. I would have been interested to learn what additional information these papers would have given to aid in the completion of the tale of this unique venture. I respected the librarian's integrity in honoring such restrictions, and I decided to proceed without seeing these particular papers. There was no alternative but to go to other sources in a further attempt to complete the picture.

Sometimes it becomes necessary to find a substitute for a personal visit to distant sources. A letter of inquiry may yield surprising results. A chance remark of a friend led me to write to the Marine Historical Society in Virginia to make inquiry about the possibility of locating a photograph of the S.S. *Continental,* the vessel on which the Mercer party voyaged west. A prompt reply directed me to the Steamship Historical Society. This latter organization not only had a fine photograph of the ship but graciously had a copy made for me, asking nothing in return but a copy of the book when it was published. Although there were many family portraits in existence, none could positively be identified as that of Conant by his living descendants.

At the Oregon Historical Society I found a single letter which Asa Mercer wrote in 1865 to Addison C. Gibbs, the Governor of Oregon, asking Gibbs if the state of Oregon would cooperate in accepting some of the the women Mercer hoped to bring west. It was disappointing when I was unsuccessful in finding Gibbs's reply.

Gradually the pieces fitted together, with here and there an empty space which served only as an incentive for further research. Now and then materials served to clarify and verify. At the University of Washington I found a few copies of *Social Voices,* a religious tract published in San Francisco and on the editorial board of which Conant served. Later I found other copies at [the] Bancroft Library, and they nicely supplemented the first group. In this paper were published excerpts of the Conant journal, excerpts similar to those Conant sent to the *New York Times.*

I found it less expensive to buy microfilm of many months of a newspaper, copies of which were not on file in the West, rather than travel to the eastern depositories to examine them. On one occasion I even prevailed upon my son-in-law to read a few months of the Boston *Commonwealth* for me. These particular issues did not seem to be on microfilm anywhere, and as he was in Cambridge, Massachusetts, for a time, he consented to do so. The resulting news items added much to my book.

Manuscript collections and historical archives are treasure troves for the researcher. There is, of course, no way of knowing what riches are hidden in a collection of personal papers, correspondence, scrapbooks, recorded interviews, diaries, and unpublished biographical sketches. The hope and excitement of finding some pertinent and hitherto unpublished material lures one on and on.

It is perhaps by now apparent that an editing task such as mine can be likened to a jig-saw puzzle wherein each piece fits into its proper place to result ultimately in a completed picture. Seldom can one find each piece because there are inevitably a few bits of needed information that elude the searcher. A few "jigs" and some "saws" remain obscure. Sometimes it is not until the work has been published that an important bit of the picture emerges from hiding. Several months after the publishing of *Mercer's Belles* I met a woman who was the grand-niece of Annie Connor, one of the Mercer Girls. She had known this aunt and had in her possession a diary which Annie kept while en route west. I am still eagerly awaiting an opportunity to read this diary. One wonders how her account of events compared with or differed from that of Conant.

Irrespective of what might be found in the future, my experience in editing the Conant journal confirms for me the thesis of Walter Webb in his presidential address before the American Historical Association in 1958, namely that history can be high adventure.

BIBLIOGRAPHY

Books

Allibone, S. Austin. *Dictionary of Authors-Supplement.* Vol. I. Philadelphia: J. B. Lippincott Co., 1896.

American Annual Cyclopedia for 1865. New York: D. Appleton and Co., 1868.

American Annual Cyclopedia for 1866. New York: D. Appleton and Co., 1873.

American Lloyd's Registry of American and Foreign Shipping. No. 159. New York: Compiled for T. D. Taylor, R. T. Hartshorne, and J. F. H. King, 1870.

Bagley, C. B. *History of Seattle.* 2 vols. Chicago: The S. J. Clarke Publishing Company, 1916, Vol. II.

Bass, Sophie Frye. *Pigtail Days in Old Seattle.* Portland, Ore.: Metropolitan Press, 1937.

_____. *When Seattle Was a Village.* Seattle: Lowman & Hanford Company, 1947.

Binns, Archie. *Northwest Gateway.* Garden City, N.Y.: Doubleday, Doran and Co., 1941.

Blankenship, G. E. *Thurston County Pioneer Reminiscences.* Olympia: Mrs. G. E. Blankenship, 1914.

Brown, Dee. *The Gentle Tamers: Women of the Old Wild West.* New York: G. P. Putnam's Sons, 1958.

Business Directory for the City of Seattle for the Year 1876. Seattle: Ward and Northrup, 1876.

California Blue Book, 1907. Sacramento: C. F. Curry, compiler, n.d.

Classified Business Directory for Santa Cruz, E. Santa Cruz, Watsonville, &c. San Francisco: California Directory Company, 1904-5.

Curtis, W. E. *Capitals of Spanish America.* New York: Harper and Bros., 1888.

Delacour, Jean. *Waterfowl of the World.* Charles Scribner's Sons, 1954.

Dictionary of American Biography. New York: Charles Scribner and Sons, 1930.

Directory of Seattle. Seattle: R. D. Pitt, 1879.

Directory of Seattle City and King County. Portland, Ore.: C. H. McIsaac, 1885-86.

Gazetteer of the World. Philadelphia: J. B. Lippincott, 1906.

Hanford, C. H. *Seattle and Environs.* Chicago and Seattle: Pioneer Historical Publishing Co., 1924.

Hawthorne, Julian. *History of Washington.* New York: American Historical Publishing Co., 1893.

Herschel, Sir John F. *Outlines of Astronomy.* New York: P. E. Collier and Son, 1901.

Holbrook, Stewart. *A Yankee Exodus.* New York: Macmillan Co., 1950.

Huntoon, D. T. V. *Philip Hunton and His Descendants.* Canton, Mass.: Cambridge University Press, 1881.

Kidder, D. P. and Fletcher, J. C. *Brazil and the Brazilians.* Philadelphia: Childs and Peterson, 1857.

Lewis' and Dryden's Marine History of the Pacific Northwest. Edgar Wilson Wright, ed. Portland, Ore.: Lewis and Dryden, 1895.

Matthews, F. C. *American Merchant Ships 1850-1890.* Salem, Mass.: Marine Research Society, 1930.

Meany, E. S. *History of the State of Washington.* New York: The Macmillan Co., 1910.

Mercer, A. S. *Washington Territory: the Great Northwest.* Utica, N.Y.: L. C. Childs, 1865.

Modern Eclectic Dictionary. New York: Colliers, 1905.

Morgan, Murray. *Skid Road.* New York: Viking Press, 1951.

New Century Cyclopedia of Names. New York: Appleton, Century, Crofts, 1954.

Oxford Dictionary of Quotations. London, New York, and Toronto: Oxford University Press, 1953.

Pacific Business Directory. San Francisco: Langley, 1867.

Prosch, Charles. *Reminiscences of Washington Territory.* Seattle: C. Prosch, 1904.

Puget Sound Business Directory. Olympia: Murphey and Harned, 1872-82.

Puget Sound Directory. Olympia: R. L. Polk, 1887.

Rathbun, J. C. *History of Thurston County.* Olympia: J. C. Rathbun, 1895.

Reclus, E. *The Earth and Its Inhabitants, South America.* Vol. II. New York: D. Appleton and Company, 1895.

Rucker, Helen. *Cargo of Brides.* Boston: Little Brown and Co., 1956.

San Francisco Directory. San Francisco: H. G. Langley, 1868.

Shenstone, N. A. *Ancedotes of Henry Ward Beecher.* Chicago: R. R. Donelley and Sons, 1887.

Thurston's Business and Resident Directory, 1912-13. Santa Cruz, Calif.: Howe's, *ca.* 1912.

Watt, Roberta Frye. *4 Wagons West.* Portland Ore.: Metropolitan Press, 1931.

_____. *The Story of Seattle.* Seattle: Lowman and Hanford Company, 1931.

Wilgus, A. Curtis. *The Development of Hispanic America.* New York: Farrar and Rinehart, 1941.

Periodicals

Bagley, C. B. "The Mercer Immigration." *Oregon Historical Quarterly,* V (1904), 1-24.

Carstensen, Vernon. "Two Letters Concerning the Mercer Girls," *Pacific Northwest Quarterly,* XXXV (1944), 343-47.

Conant, Roger. "The Cruise of the Continental," *Social Voices,* I, II, III (1867, 1868, 1869).

Draper, Benjamin. "Dogs, Earthquakes and Emperors," *American Heritage,* I (1950), 28.

"Emigration to Washington of 400 on the Steamer 'Continental,' " with drawing by A. R. Waud. *Harper's Weekly Magazine,* X (1866), 8, 9.

Engle, Flora Pearson. "The Story of the Mercer Expedition," *Washington Historical Quarterly,* VI (1915), 225-37.

Gabriel, John. "How Washington Got Its Women," *Evergreen Magazine,* I (1946), 14, 33, 34.

Henderson, Delphine. "Asa Shinn Mercer, Northwest Publicity Agent," *Reed College Bulletin,* XXIII (1945), 26.
Holbrook, Stewart. "Mercer's Maids for Marriage," *Woman's Day Magazine,* XI (1948), 46, 47, 80, 89-93.
Hyland, T. S. "Around the Horn to Matrimony," *American Mercury,* LV (1942), 480-85.
Jump, E. "Mercer's Belles," *Puck, the Pacific Pictorial,* II (1866), cartoon tipped in.
Meany, E. S. "Early Records of the University," *Washington Historical Quarterly,* VIII (1917), 114-23.
Smith, Charles W. "Asa Shinn Mercer, Pioneer in Western Publicity," *Pacific Northwest Quarterly,* XXVII (1936), 347-55.

Manuscripts

Andrews, L. W. B. Letter, Olympia, Washington, December 18, 1865, to C. B. Bagley. In Bagley Collection of Letters, 1861-79, University of Washington Library.
Bogart, N. M. "Reminiscences of Early Pioneer Days." Typed MS in Sophie Frye Bass Library, Seattle Historical Society.
Booth, M. S. (King County Auditor). Letter, n.d., to Reverend John F. Damon, Misc. Folder in Bagley Collection of Letters, University of Washington Library.
Brown, Mrs. Amos (Anna Peebles). Typed interview, *ca.* 1914, in Sophie Frye Bass Library, Seattle Historical Society.
Carey, F. J. Letter, Los Angeles, March 7, 1956, to Lenna Deutsch.
Carr, J. Tyler. Letter, San Francisco, September 8, 1866, to C. B. Bagley. Bagley Collection of Letters, 1861-79, University of Washington Library.
Kernighan, Nina I. MS in Washington State Historical Society Library.
MacIntosh, Mrs. Angus (Libbie Peebles). Typed interview, *ca.* 1914, in Sophie Frye Bass Library, Seattle Historical Society.
Mercer, Asa Shinn. Letter, Olympia, June 2, 1864, to Governor Addison C. Gibbs. In Gibbs Papers, Oregon Historical Society Library.
Osborne, E. S. Interview, n.d. University of Washington Library.
Pearson, Daniel. "Family Records and Reminiscences of Washington Pioneers." Vol. II. Typed, bound MS compiled by the D.A.R., *ca.* 1929-30. In Eastern Washington Historical Society Library.
Pearson, D. C. Letter, Seattle, May 22, 1957, to Lenna Deutsch.
Pinkham, Ida May Barlow. "Family Records and Reminiscences of Washington Pioneers." Typed, bound MS compiled by the D.A.R., *ca* 1929-30. In Eastern Washington Historical Society Library.
Poland, Mrs. Helen Loud. Interview with Lenna Deutsch, July, 1954.
Webster, Mrs. David (Sarah Robinson). Interview, *ca.* 1914, in Sophie Frye Bass Library, Seattle Historical Society.

Newspapers

Alta California (San Francisco). 1865; 1866; 1867; 1873.
Boston Evening Courier. July 27, 1865.
Boston Evening Transcript. January 19, 1866.
The British Columbian (New Westminster, B.C.). 1865; 1882.
Calaveras Chronicle (Mokelumne Hill, Calif.). April 28, 1866.

The Colonist (Victoria, B.C.). 1862; 1863; 1865; 1866.

Commonwealth (Boston). June 30, 1865; September 9, 1865; October 28, 1865.

Herald (Boston). June 30, 1865.

Idaho World (Idaho City). September 9, 1865; October 28, 1865.

Morning Call (San Francisco). January 4, 1867.

Morning Oregonian (Portland, Ore.). 1865; 1866; June 13, 1889; May 7, 1893; August 10, 1913; May 31, 1942.

Mountaineer (The Dalles, Ore.). September 6, 1865.

New York Daily Tribune. October 6, 1865; December 14, 1865.

New York Herald. 1865.

New York Times. 1865-68.

Northwestern Live Stock Journal (Cheyenne, Wyo.). July 11, 1885.

Oregon Sentinel (Jacksonville). February 10, 1866.

Oregon Statesman (Salem). October, 1865; July 2, 1866.

Pacific Tribune (Olympia, W.T.). September 23, 1865; April 28, 1866.

Post-Intelligencer (Seattle). November, December, 1915; March, April, 1916; May, 1919; January, 1955.

Puget Sound Daily (Seattle). 1865; 1866.

Puget Sound Herald (Steilacoom). 1861; 1862; 1864.

Puget Sound Weekly (Seattle). May, June, 1866.

Sacramento Daily Union. March 28, 1856; April 4, 1856; April 18, 1856; June 26, 1856; September, 1865; April, May, 1866; February 19, 1878.

San Francisco Examiner. June 23, 1893.

San Francisco Mercury. November 17, 1867.

Santa Cruz Sentinel (Santa Cruz, Calif.). May, 1870-May 1879.

Seattle Daily Times. January 10, 1943; January 19, 1948; August 15, 1951.

Seattle Gazette. 1864; 1865; 1866.

Seattle Star. May 24, 1947.

Sunday Olympian (Olympia). August 17, 1910.

Sunday Times (Seattle). November 8, 1903; July-October, 1951.

Tacoma Daily Ledger. August 24, 1913.

Vancouver Daily Post (Victoria, B.C.). September, October, 1865.

Vancouver Register (Vancouver, W.T.). 1865; 1866.

Victoria Daily Chronicle. June 6, 1866.

Walla Walla Statesman. September, October, 1865; March, 1866.

Washington Democrat (Olympia, W.T.). 1864, 1865.

Washington Standard (Olympia, W.T.). 1865; 1866.

Wilbur Register (Wilbur, Wash.). November, 1939.

INDEX